A TRAIL OF TWO TELEGRAPHS

A TRAIL OF TWO TELEGRAPHS

And Other Historic Tales of the Bulkley Valley and Beyond

JANE STEVENSON

CAITLIN PRESS
HALFMOON BAY, BC

01 02 03 04 05 06 18 17 16 15 14 13

Caitlin Press Inc.
8100 Alderwood Road, Halfmoon Bay, BC, V0N 1Y1 | www.caitlin-press.com

Text design by Kathleen Fraser.
Cover design by Vici Johnstone.
Edited by Catherine Edwards.
Map by Hans Saefkow.
Printed in Canada.

Caitlin Press Inc. acknowledges financial support from the Government of Canada through the Canada Book Fund and the Canada Council for the Arts, and from the Province of British Columbia through the British Columbia Arts Council and the Book Publisher's Tax Credit.

Canada Council   Conseil des arts
for the Arts   du Canada

BRITISH COLUMBIA
ARTS COUNCIL
An agency of the Province of British Columbia

Library and Archives Canada Cataloguing in Publication

Stevenson, Jane, 1977–
    A trail of two telegraphs : and other historic tales of the
Bulkley Valley and beyond / Jane Stevenson.

Includes bibliographical references and index.
ISBN 978-1-927575-02-4

    1. Frontier and pioneer life—British Columbia, Northern.
2. British Columbia, Northern—History. 3. British Columbia,
Northern—Biography. I. Title.

FC3845.B78S74 2013   971.1'82   C2013-900599-4

This collection is dedicated to Joanne Campbell, the awesome publisher of Northword Magazine—*where most of these stories were first shared.*

A Note about First Nations

Readers will notice a lack of First Nations stories in this book. I am very aware of the significant heritage sites, interesting legends and numerous active First Nations groups in this area. Yet I chose not to present these stories here. This was done out of respect for the First Nations traditions because I feel their stories are theirs to tell.

CONTENTS

Above, left to right: Members of the RCMP Tactical Unit, June 12, 1976, courtesy of Kitimat Museum and Archives, Northern Sentinel Press Collection; one of Cataline's pack trains, courtesy of Bulkley Valley Museum, P0336; April 7, 1914: railway workers race toward the last spike, courtesy of Bulkley Valley Museum, P0345; 1913: a farmer plows a field at Hubert east of Telkwa, courtesy of Bulkley Valley Museum, P0021; Wally West photo of *Vancouver Daily Province* newspaper carrier Walter Webster, courtesy of the Exploration Place, Wally West Collection, N1993.11.1.797; First Nations canoes travel the Skeena River from the coast, courtesy of Telkwa Museum, P0160.

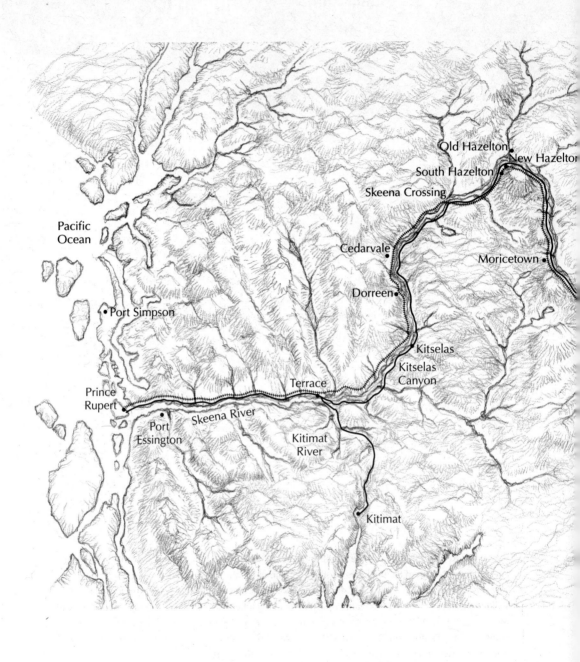

Pacific
Ocean

Old Hazelton
New Hazelton
South Hazelton
Skeena Crossing
Cedarvale
Moricetown
Port Simpson
Dorreen
Kitselas
Kitselas
Canyon
Terrace
Prince
Rupert
Skeena River
Port
Essington
Kitimat
River
Kitimat

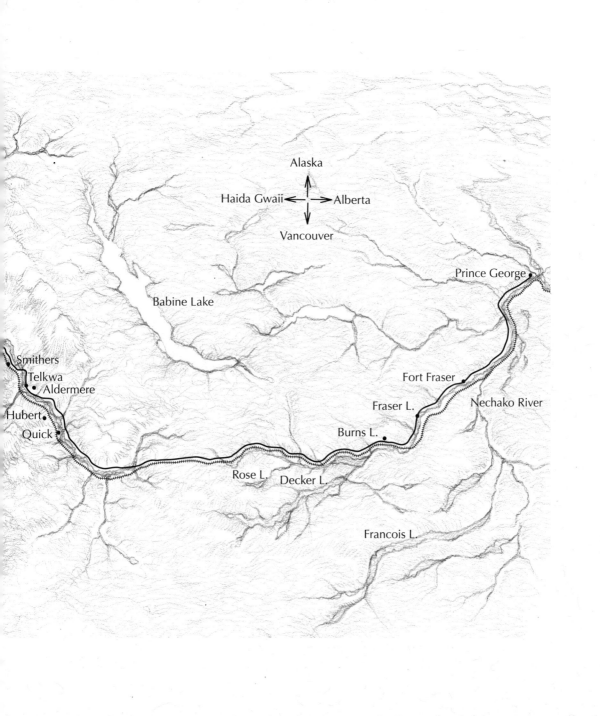

Alaska

Haida Gwaii ⟵✦⟶ Alberta

Vancouver

Prince George

Babine Lake

Smithers
Telkwa
Aldermere

Hubert
Quick

Fort Fraser

Nechako River

Fraser L.

Burns L.

Rose L.   Decker L.

Francois L.

INTRODUCTION

I was born in St. Lawrence, Newfoundland. My parents moved our family to Kitimat, British Columbia, when I was a baby. I grew up in Kitimat, a small town on the north coast of British Columbia, and every few years my siblings and I accompanied our mother "home" to Newfoundland for a visit.

In Newfoundland we were surrounded by many aunts, uncles, cousins—there were houses that had been in our family for generations, personal stories that were part of the rocky cliffs and the beaches, and entire sections of old graveyards contained relatives. Family in Newfoundland could spout out historical facts, ramble off birth dates and entertain with historical tales.

Back in Kitimat our family formed a relationship with our town and northern BC. We explored the mountains and back roads in the Kitimat Valley; we learned to name mountain ranges and creeks. We found remains of the original smelter site settlement and walked through sacred Haisla burial grounds. My dad never drove past an interpretive plaque without stopping. My siblings and I may have been reluctant historians, but we did learn the facts. On my parents' bookshelf I found and read Elizabeth Anderson Varley's *Kitimat, My Valley* and Gordon Robinson's *Tales of Kitimaat*.

I graduated from high school and moved away from my family and siblings in Kitimat. My first job after graduating from the University of Victoria was at the

Bulkley Valley Museum in Smithers. There I met Elders with a long-time personal connection to place who generously shared tales with me. As I catalogued photographs, cared for old papers, ledgers and journals, as I created exhibits and answered research requests, I learned. I learned many interesting historical stories about the Bulkley Valley and beyond that I wish I had known years ago.

I wanted to share the stories of interesting characters, fantastic feats and important events. Thanks to *Northword Magazine* I found my chance to reach locals and travellers along Highway 16 by writing historical articles once every two months for the last five years. Thanks to Caitlin Press, these stories and additional historical tales can now reach even further. It is my hope that the following stories about personal triumphs and little-known interesting events and significant people and places can help connect people to this place: so we all have a richer sense of this area—the Bulkley Valley and beyond.

SKEENA FORKS

It was Simon McGillivray who, in a letter to George Simpson dated July 15, 1833, first advocated for the Hudson's Bay Company to establish a post at the confluence of the Skeena River and the Bulkley River. McGillivray stood at the fork of the rivers without a map and without an accurate idea of how the river systems flowed—he mistakenly referred to the Skeena as the Nass River and used the original name, the Wetsonqua River, for the Bulkley River. McGillivray had been sent to look for ways to improve trade to and from the coast and was told by his First Nations guides that from where they stood on June 21, 1833, at the confluence of the Bulkley and Skeena Rivers, a canoe could reach the coast in a few days.

It wasn't until 1866 that the Hudson's Bay Company sent two men who were already in the Skeena River area, Thomas Hankin and William Manson, to establish a small trading post and general store at the Skeena Forks to assess the trade routes and also to take advantage of selling goods to the gold seekers and telegraph construction crews that were increasingly travelling through the area. But just two years after opening, in 1868, the small Hudson's Bay Company post at Hazelton was closed with the company claiming that the post hadn't brought in a significant enough profit. Pioneer Hankin must have sensed a business opportunity, because he left the Hudson's Bay Company with the closure of the Hazelton Post and decided to stay on in the area. Hankin teamed up with Robert Cunningham and together they opened their own store and liquor dispensary near Gitanmaax. He

A sternwheeler pulled up to the banks of the Skeena River at Hazelton. Photo courtesy of Bulkley Valley Museum, P1470.

no doubt saw that the Skeena Forks was becoming a frequent stopping place for the travellers all months of the year—the surveyors and miners and their pack animals. This was also the time when the Collins Overland Telegraph project was abandoned and some of those men stayed on and built cabins in Hazelton. With their pioneering store, Cunningham and Hankin attempted to supply the travelling prospectors and occasional settler with some goods brought up the Skeena River by canoe freighters in the summer or by dog team in the winter.

The trails connecting the newly established Hazelton community with the Babine and Omenica District and the Nass and the Coastal District were well-travelled trails but not convenient for pack animals. Dr. Large writes in his book,

Skeena: River of Destiny, that in 1871 Robert Cunningham from the fort at Port Simpson and Thomas Hankin were contracted by the provincial government to improve the trail between Gitanmaax and Babine Lake—the route the miners took and a long-time trail for the area First Nations. The prospectors had voiced complaints to the province about the narrow trail and the fallen trees that frequently blocked the path. Travellers became weary clearing trail for the pack animals and some who were ill prepared for the long and difficult work became disheartened and abandoned the trip; worse still, some naive travellers even lost their lives. There was a whole crew of men working on improving the trail who completed it just in time for the Skeena gold rush of 1871 and 1872.

"In 1871," writes Large, "there were six buildings and a tent in Hazelton." But more stores were soon constructed and permanent homes went up among the temporary shacks. In the March 1872 *British Colonist,* an ad for the Farron and Mitchell Store at Skeena Forks boasted, "Miners and others bound for the Omenica will find groceries, provisions and complete outfits at our store. Having 20,000 pounds of bacon already at the Forks we can sell it cheaper than it can be brought in from Victoria." Also in 1872, a letter appeared in Victoria's *British Colonist* from "Hazelnut." The anonymous letter writer describes Hazelton as a town "situated on the west bank of the Skeena about one mile from the forks of the Wetsonqua [Bulkley River], on a large level hazel flat from which it has taken its name." Hazelnut goes on to say there are now ten large well-built stores and houses beside small dwelling houses. Hazelnut writes that, "our gardens look splendid and not less than 20 tons of potatoes and at least 10 tons of turnips, besides other vegetables will be the result." The Hudson's Bay Company saw the successes of Cunningham and Hankin—not only could supplies get to the forks of the Skeena but there were people there to buy them—and the company decided to reopen in 1880.

A Skeena River survey was carried out in 1890 for the Hudson's Bay Company. The surveyor, Captain George Odin, recommended navigating the Skeena River with sternwheelers. In 1891, the sternwheeler *Caledonia* was built and made the first successful trip to the forks of the Skeena at Hazelton in the same year. The

The houses and stores of early Hazelton. Photo courtesy of Bulkley Valley Museum, P1930.

Hazelton, B.C.
M.Rae Bros

steamboat era changed Hazelton—the settlement became permanent, and it flour-
ished. As the Hazelton Pioneer Museum information display states, "it was a vital
centre of activity for prospectors, traders, merchants, pack train operators and
missionaries." The Skeena River may have been very difficult to navigate by
sternwheeler, but the new transportation mode meant more freight and more passengers for Hazelton.

One of the many new settlers in Hazelton was Mr. F.C. Chettleburgh, who
arrived in 1909. In an interview recorded in 1962, Chettleburgh recalls his journey
up the Skeena River to Hazelton. Chettleburgh travelled aboard the sternwheeler
Port Simpson and experienced "rapture" caused by the towering mountains, the
hardy settlers and the First Nations people. "In those days," said Chettleburgh,
"Hazelton had about fifty or sixty whites and an equal number, if not more, of
Indians living up on the bench. And the Indian dogs, there must have been a
hundred and fifty if not more, living under the sidewalks in Hazelton, near the
cafes and the hotels." Chettleburgh lists off various businesses in early Hazelton:
three hotels, the Hudson's Bay Company post, Sargent's store, Larkworthy's store,
a jeweller, a watchmaker, a photographic shop, a bank, the newspaper and the
Hazelton Hospital. It was a bustling little town. And noisy—the many loose dogs
would howl and bark in response to the whistle of the sternwheelers as they pulled
in and departed from the banks of the Skeena River.

The Hazelton Pioneer Museum and Archives states that between 1890 and
1915 Hazelton was the largest community in northwestern British Columbia.
Chettleburgh summarizes his impressions of these years and the people who lived
in Hazelton after 1909 and later, in early Telkwa. He says, "What made that
country, and when I say that country I mean the Bulkley Valley, the Omenica...
more than anything else, in spite of the fact many that came up there were very
green, was as long as they played ball, and did the right thing, and paid up their
debts, they were always brothers. They always helped one another out. And that's
the remarkable thing about that country, how they stood behind one another. It
helped to build up the character in the young fellas and those that couldn't take
the rough spots, they naturally had to get out." The little community on the

ROCHER DE BOULE, HAZELTON. B.C   PHOTO W.WW   1911

Wiggs O'Neill's vessel, *Kitexchan*, "people of the big river." This launch was taken overland to Aldermere and on to Francois Lake. Photo courtesy of Bulkley Valley Museum, P0747.

banks of the Skeena River grew from the trading post that Simon McGillivray first imagined in 1833 to a bustling community by 1890, and remains today as Hazelton, a permanent community of very proud locals.

TWO TELEGRAPHS

Every spring since 2007 Ryan Holmes and Jim Foulkes have slashed their way through thorny devil's club and battled thirsty mosquitoes in search of buried strands of wire, the remains of a shelter, or the telltale blue glass insulators from the Collins Overland Telegraph—the line that connected BC to the world in 1866.

The Collins Overland Telegraph represented Mr. Perry Collins' ambitious goal in 1864 to connect North America with Europe via telegraph. The $3 million project aimed to lay telegraph wire across the western US to New Westminster, BC, then north to Quesnel and west to Hazelton—crossing 850 miles of British Columbia before then crossing the Bering Sea and spanning 1,800 miles of Russia. Several unsuccessful attempts had been made to lay a telegraph cable across the Atlantic between Newfoundland and the UK, but Perry Collins and many other investors thought the transatlantic cable had little chance of permanent success.

The Collins Overland Telegraph project was a massive undertaking, and run with military precision. Uniformed men had strict roles and clear orders from US Army Colonel Charles S. Bulkley, the project's engineer-in-chief.

By the summer of 1865, the telegraph crew had completed a line as far as Quesnel and had struggled through the bush, clearing right-of-way, as far north and west as Fort Fraser. The men drove their own herd of beef cattle and two hundred

Wagons travel a section of the telegraph trail between Decker Lake and Moricetown. The poles with glass insulators and telegraph wire are visible on the left side. Photo courtesy Bulkley Valley Museum, P0601.

pack animals. In the spring of 1866, one hundred and fifty men blazed a trail, built log cabins and strung telegraph wire out of Quesnel northwest to the confluence of the Bulkley and Skeena Rivers. There they met with the men who had toiled up the Skeena in canoes laden with hundreds of pounds of supplies and telegraph wire.

Together, the land team and the river team cleared the twelve- to twenty-foot-wide right-of-way, constructed bridges, graded slopes, built cabins and strung telegraph wire to the village of Kispiox. Here the men built Fort Stager, where they stored 240 miles of wire, insulators and brackets. By winter twenty-five miles of line had been built northwest of Fort Stager and work was expected to resume in the spring of 1867.

But work never resumed. Unbeknownst to the workers, the transatlantic cable had proven itself in the summer of 1866. This was the end of the Collins Overland Telegraph, and no further work was done on the line after the winter of

Those telegraph cabins that still remain are well on their way to returning to the earth. This telegraph cabin is near Bell II, northwest of Hazelton. Photo by Ken Newman.

1866. S.A. Cunliffe, in *From Pack Trail to Radio and Then What?*, stated that in 1868 Mr. McCutcheon, an operator, abandoned Fort Stager, bringing out with him thirteen large canoes loaded with provisions and clothing. Rosemary Neering, in her book *Continental Dash*, writes, "The Company [Western Union Telegraph] maintained the line from New Westminster to the Cariboo... until 1871 when the provincial government leased the line in perpetuity."

When gold was discovered in the Yukon in 1891, the world wanted to know all about it. The federally owned Dominion Telegraph Services began work in 1897, intent on resurrecting the old Collins Overland Telegraph line that ran out of Quesnel to Kispiox and then branched off towards Kuldo and ran overland to Telegraph Creek and the Yukon. They built thirty-seven cabins—one every thirty or forty miles. Two men were stationed to a cabin: a telegraph operator and a lineman. The lineman would patrol the line on either side of the cabin, repairing it when it had been broken by falling trees, wind or heavy snows. Because they were responsible for a long section of line, there were refuge cabins built at the halfway points with a bed, a stove and provisions. Due to extreme weather (like the ten feet of snow that fell in one day at the head of the Nass River), some linemen also built an additional shelter between the refuge cabin and their main cabin. By the fall of 1901, the line was complete and Dawson City was connected via telegraph to the rest of the world.

That first winter, 1901, was the hardest, the men having underestimated their supplies and the duration of the winter weather. At first the pack trains (with some seventy-five animals) that supplied the cabins were sent out annually, but due to near-starvation they soon operated more frequently. Conditions along the line were tough: the men battled forest fires, spring floods and week-long blizzards. The work was hard; some claimed to have walked three hundred miles in just one month as they constantly repaired their sections of line.

There were the inevitable reports of fist-fights, men going stir-crazy, and even a shoot-out. One lineman, desperate to get farther away from his co-worker, built his own cabin next door. Former lineman S.A. Cunliffe wrote of a man murdered over the position of the salt shaker on the table.

In spite of the hardships, some who had come intending to stay just one season instead stayed for years. Most of the men played cards and some played musical instruments. Companionship was found in their pack dogs, the daily 8:00 pm roll call and the repeating of the daily news headlines. The mailman, who walked or mushed the route, became an important link to the outside world. The linemen helped out the occasional traveller and were known to rustle up a rescue team, provide shelter in emergencies and literally give the shirt off their back to a stranger in need.

For the more than thirty years the line was maintained, the telegraph linemen changed but the routine was the same: they maintained the line and passed news along the wire, relaying the signals from cabin to cabin.

Marcella Love and an Insulator Discovery

In Smithers, British Columbia, a sea-foam blue insulator is the pride of Marcella Love's collection.

Marcella Edmonds was fifteen in 1942 when her mother, father and sisters moved to Smithers, BC, from Alberta. Marcella and her sisters enjoyed Smithers. Over the years she found work at Goodacre's grocery store, the Royal Bank and the Hanson Lumber and Timber Company. Marcella met well-known and respected Kispiox guide Wally Love at a dance. As Marcella says, "it was love at first sight, in more ways than one." They were married in 1951. Marcella and Wally lived on a ranch in the Kispiox Valley, where together they raised two daughters, Lois and Lorna.

One day Wally Love was guiding through the Kispiox Valley when his horse kicked up a perfect blue glass insulator. Marcella says, "he thought I might like it and just dropped it in his pack saddle for me." Years later Marcella learned the insulator dated back to the Collins Overland Telegraph expedition of 1866, and was so old that it lacked the threaded core built into later insulators. It survived decades buried in the ground, was kicked up by a horse and bounced around in a pack saddle, yet is one of the few known Collins Overland insulators in perfect condition. Love's windowsill may exhibit a bright line of clear glass and white ceramic insulators yet she doesn't think of herself as a serious collector. She values the Collins Overland Telegraph insulator for its personal history and as a physical reminder of her husband Wally and the happy times they spent with their two young daughters in the Kispiox Valley.

During a spring flood in 1936, a large portion of the line between Hazelton and Telegraph Creek was washed out. Since radio communication had begun by this time, the decision was made to not rebuild the telegraph line to the Yukon.

The linemen dispersed, the cabins fell into disrepair, the forest grew over the poles and wires, and the once twelve-foot-wide trail steadily grew in. The old poles were taken over by the wilderness, but there are discoveries of old wires under the layers of leaves and glass insulators turn up with ground disturbances.

A report by the Kitimat Stikine Regional District states that the telegraph trail to the Yukon is valued for "... its scientific and engineering feats, which included the physical construction of the trail and telegraph line through difficult terrain, developments in communications technology of the time, and the physical presence of a continuous wire through the wilderness." The report notes "... the use of the trail by many diverse people over time including First Nations, prospectors, trappers, packers and outlaws adds to its social and cultural significance."

Some push for the trail to be officially designated a heritage trail, mapped and marked and promoted as a hiking route through the wilderness. Jim Foulkes and Ryan Holmes appreciate the heritage significance of the telegraph trail to northern British Columbia; if they do find the end of the Collins line, they will GPS it, photograph it and share the information with local and provincial museums. The Regional District plans to commemorate the telegraph line with an interpretive plaque. Holmes and Foulkes would like to see a rock cairn established at the historic end of the line. Foulkes says that the telegraph route, both the early Collins and the later Dominion lines, are monuments to the vision these people had to link BC with the world more than a hundred and forty years ago.

HORETZKY'S HIKE ACROSS

NORTHERN BC

Despite dire warnings of thick brush, massive swamps and impassable mountain ranges, explorer Charles Horetzky was determined to walk from northern Alberta to Fort Simpson (Lax Kw'alaams) at the mouth of the Nass River on BC's Pacific coast. He packed nine horses with 230 pounds of flour, 12 pounds of tea, 24 pounds of sugar, 150 pounds of pemmican and other supplies. On September 2, 1872, along with botanist Dr. John Macoun and two guides, he left Fort Edmonton.

Charles Horetzky, then thirty-four years old, had arrived in Fort Edmonton as the official photographer for Sir Sanford Fleming's cross-country survey crew from Upper Fort Garry (now Winnipeg, Manitoba). Despite having taken stunning photographs on that journey, Horetzky was cut loose at Edmonton: Fleming sent him on a mission to walk through the mountains, over difficult terrain, to the coast of northern British Columbia—in the winter. He was told to verify the elevation of the Peace River Pass, to record descriptions of north-central BC, and to see if the route would be a possibility for the proposed transcontinental railway. Others might have balked at the great distance, the approaching winter, the unknown... but Horetzky took on the challenge and travelled from Fort

Edmonton to Fort Simpson in the winter of 1872–73. He photographed his journey and kept a journal, leaving behind a dramatic account of his travels.

Canada on the Pacific: Being an Account of a Journey from Edmonton to the Pacific by the Peace River Valley tells the story of Horetzky's travels to Fort Simpson. Horetzky and his group travelled through northern Alberta towards the BC border, encountered a grizzly bear, accidentally started a small wildfire, and eventually abandoned their cart and most of the horses due to the difficult terrain. In early October they arrived in Dunvegan, continued to Fort St. John, and travelled on to the Rocky Mountain Portage. It was in the Rockies that Horetzky learned of another pass, the Pine Pass. The First Nations people told him this route would be the best choice for a railway or a road through the mountains.

Horetzky and his companions canoed the Parsnip, Peace and McLeod Rivers to McLeod Lake, arrived at Fort McLeod on November 5. Horetzky used dogs to carry his gear eighteen miles in eight days to Fort St. James on Stuart Lake. Here Dr. Macoun left the group and headed to Victoria with his rattling tin plant-presses full of samples. On December 2, Horetzky restocked flour, tea, sugar and "… the dietary institution of British Columbia—bacon and beans." Horetzky wrote that he and his three First Nations guides "very reluctantly resumed our weary tramp, which was to cease at whatever point on the coast we might be lucky enough to find the Hudson's Bay Company steamship, the *Otter*."

Horetzky described his path to Babine Lake as difficult, "during which slips and falls were the rule and upright walking was the exception." His camps were wretched, with far too many uncomfortable, to be exact, "angular beds." There was too little snow that winter for snowshoes and for many of the miles, Horetzky and companions were forced to walk through the snow and wade through the occasional deep drifts. They arrived at the shores of Babine Lake on December 10 to find the lake still open. This came as a great disappointment because the travellers were hoping to make good time by walking on the ice down the lake to the fort. On the edge of the thin-iced shoreline, Horetzky came upon a "wretched apology" for a canoe. The canoe leaked and was so unsteady they were almost tossed out more than once.

"About three miles from Hazelton and three hundred feet down in the rocky bed of the Wetsonqua [Bulkley River] here is a large Indian village called Achwlget. Immediately in front of it the Indians have thrown a suspension bridge across a rocky chasm. The bridge is built entirely of wood fastened together by withes and branches; its height above the roaring waters beneath is fifty feet and it sways about under the weight of a man." December 1872, Horetzky's journal. Photo by Horetzky, courtesy of Bulkley Valley Museum, P1453.

The men, who had, as Horetzky stated, "excessively depressing spirits," managed to make their way down the lake and survive the sudden gusts of winds and large swells. At Fort Babine they rested and two new First Nation guides were hired, one of whom was recommended as a master of the French language. "I found out afterwards," wrote Horetzky, "his sole vocabulary consisted of the adverbs *oui* and *non* which he used at every possible occasion, regardless of consequence." Horetzky nicknamed this man "the linguist" and judged both the First Nations guides to be "active and willing." They left Fort Babine on December 15 and walked through the Suskwa Pass to Hazelton. Horetzky noted, "the path was rough with numerous deep ravines, necessitating laborious ascents and descents; great care was taken over their steep and icy sides."

Just before midnight on December 18, the party arrived in the community of Hazelton and were welcomed into Tom Hankin's Store and Hotel for a "homeopathic dose of hot scotch." Horetzky decided to stay in Hazelton for the Christmas celebrations, which consisted of several consecutive days and nights of festivities: a constant din of music, singing, dancing and bar fights with fireworks, muskets and revolvers firing.

Horetzky stayed at the confluence of the Bulkley and Skeena Rivers for two weeks. He explored the area, took photographs and recorded his impressions of the people and places of early Hazelton in his journal. He noted the people were jovial and reckless, and wrote that "the miners were a curious combination of pluck and endurance, although often unfortunate he is never discouraged." The stores in Hazelton restocked Horetzky with flour, bacon, beans, tea and dried salmon. He left Hazelton on January 4 with "four coast Indians who engaged with [him] at the very moderate rate of 75 cents a day." These guides spoke Chinook, and not one word of English. On their first night away from the comforts of Hazelton, the group settled down to sleep "in a spot that had [a] foreboding aspect and did not allow sufficient level space for a dog to coil up in." They passed the village of Kitselguecla, which Horetzky recorded as being deserted, with the First Nations people away to attend a feast. Farther down the trail, they met over one hundred Kitselguecla First Nations people on their way home from a feast in Kitwancool. Horetzky was greatly impressed with the strength of these people, "all men, women and children laden with large cedar boxes filled with rendered grease of the candle fish caught in the Nass waters."

The winter days were very short, and Horetzky and his guides made slow progress. "The snow is three and a half feet deep and extremely wet and soft," he wrote, but "we pushed on, the trail becoming very much worse, the barometer falling steadily, and a constant drizzle of fine hard snow totally obscuring the mountains." On January 7 they reached Kitwancool, which Horetzky recorded as being a village of about twenty large longhouses. "For the last ten days," he wrote, "this village had been the place of barter between the Nass Indians and those of the Interior."

The men continued their walk and along the trail the group encountered "Muskaboo," who guided them first to the Chean-hown (Cranberry) River, then along the Nass River. Horetzky described a part of this journey thus: "January 14:

The only time off that Horetzky had during his overland winter journey was two weeks spent in the Hazelton area over Christmas and New Year 1872. Photo by Horetzky, courtesy of Library and Archives Canada, PA022575.

we took to the river on a narrow ledge of ice upon which we very cautiously crawled two hundred yards having, on one hand, a perpendicular wall of rock, while upon the other the swift waters of the Nass seethed and boiled in a manner which actually caused blood to curdle as a single false step would have inevitably cost us our lives." Horetzky noted that Muskaboo spoke the English language very well but with a curious Yorkshire accent that made him occasionally hard to understand. Muskaboo accompanied Horetzky and his Hazelton guides to Gitwinksihlkw. Here they rested and were entertained by native dancers: "… fifty men and women participated, nearly all masked… the motions were vigorous; and if not graceful, were, at any rate whimsical, and rather free; the men and women dancing alternately. There seemed to be a leader on both sides, who did his or her utmost to execute the most fantastic steps, which were accompanied by fantastic facial contortions and a monotonous chant, with which they kept excellent time."

Horetzky and company walked on to the village of Kitawn [no longer occupied]. They were nearing the coast now and experienced rain that saturated the snow and covered the ice and generally made walking "execrable." Horetzky wrote he was "completely drenched and our snow shoes entirely used up from the effects of the water through which we had been obliged to wade for the last ten miles."

On January 20 Horetzky posted his destination as Fort Simpson and set out with eight hired First Nations men and a very fine cedar dugout canoe "of a most

The Cholera Box

In Horetzky's *Canada on the Pacific,* he mentions that while he stopped over in Hazelton in the winter of 1872–73 he took his camera and went for a trip up the "Wetsonqua" River (the Bulkley River). Horetzky was accompanied by Hazelton resident Tom Hankin, some local First Nations guides and Charlie, a "Hyder Indian" guide. Hankin told Horetzky his camera would be terrifying to the First Nations people because of an earlier outbreak of cholera in the area. "A few months previous," wrote Horetzky, "Mr. T----[Tomlinson], the gentleman in charge of the Mission Station at the mouth of the Nass had paid a pastoral visit to the Achwylget Indians [Hagwilget]." The reverend had brought with him a magic lantern and slides that were shown to the First Nations villages throughout the area. "After the reverend gentleman's departure, however," wrote Horetzky, "it most unfortunately happened that a species of cholera broke out amongst the native Hazeltonians; the origin they most illogically attributed to the one eyed devil in the lantern and its exhibitor." Hankin referred to Horetzky's camera as the "cholera box" and attributed the camera to their steady abandonment by the local First Nations guides. One morning they awoke to see that only Charlie remained. Charlie told them the others had left "in mortal terror of the box and its mysterious contents." Horetzky wrote, "Tom and I thus fell in for equal shares of the remaining load, while Charlie, being a Hyder and above such superstitious fear, shouldered the box without comment."

graceful mould, intended to stand a rough sea." For the miles of partially frozen river before they reached the open seas, the canoe was mounted on a roughly constructed sled to be pulled over the ice. The group experienced three wet, stormy days and nights in which "… heavy gusts followed each other in rapid succession, driving the pitiless rain, which soon changed to sleet and snow… every now and then a terrific gust would threaten to blow fire, tent and everything into the water. Camp making on the sea coast in the midst of a pelting rain is a very different affair from the same operation in the interior, and oh! How I wished for a temperature of twenty or thirty degrees below zero."

Finally, on January 23, 1873, Horetzky and his guides pulled the canoe onto the muddy beaches of Fort Simpson. He had reached his destination. "Several miners, on their way to the Omenica via the Nass, curious to find out who we were, stood at the beach where we landed, and in answer to their inquiry as to where we came from, they received the laconic answer, 'Fort Garry' [Winnipeg]. A stare of incredulity was returned."

Despite the winter season, the unknown route and a motley crew of guides, Horetzky successfully journeyed from Fort Edmonton, Alberta, to coastal Fort Simpson, BC—well over six hundred miles in less than five months. Upon his return to Ottawa in March 1873, Horetzky was an outspoken advocate of the Peace River Valley and the Pine Pass as the best route for Canada's first transcontinental railway. The government disagreed, and the Canadian Pacific Railway was built instead through the Kicking Horse Pass in southern BC. Later, the Grand Trunk Pacific Railway/Canadian National Railway constructed its line through the more northerly Yellowhead Pass. Before making a permanent home in Ontario, Horetzky returned to BC to survey the north coast in 1874 and the Homathko Valley in 1875. He died in 1900, leaving behind a stunning legacy of historical photographs and journals—and a little tributary of the Kemano River that he was bold enough to name after himself. Mount Horetzky, north of the Babine River, was named in 1938 by the Geological Survey of Canada to commemorate the explorer.

CATALINE

O n the edge of a hill in Gitenmaax Cemetery, there is a small rock cairn
that overlooks the confluence of the Skeena and Bulkley Rivers and has
for a backdrop the black rock face of the Roche DeBoule range. The
stone marker reads, "Jean Jacques Caux—Cataline, the packer—1830–1922."

Jean Jacques Caux was nicknamed Cataline due to the misconception he
was from Catalonia, a once-independent kingdom bordering on his birthplace
of Bearn in France. He spoke a rapid mixture of French, English, Spanish, and
Chinook jargon, the First Nations-European trade language that was common in
the Pacific Northwest at the time.

Cataline left his home country and eventually made his way to British
Columbia with other gold seekers. He drove large teams of mules and horses out
of Yale, Ashcroft, Quesnel and Barkerville during the gold rushes of 1858, 1863
and 1898. Cataline's pack trains went where wagons could not, carrying goods
and equipment through the wilderness and over difficult terrain.

As the gold rushes led to wider roads in the Cariboo, Cataline's pack trains
were no longer needed and he moved north and west into the Bulkley Valley and
the Hazeltons. He supplied the early settlers, prospectors and telegraph linemen
with much-needed supplies and had good relations with the First Nations peoples
in whose territories he travelled. Cataline's pack trains were significant in size,
employing five to six men with thirty to sixty mules carrying 250 to 300 pounds

Cairn erected by Hazelton residents. Photo courtesy of Cataline's great-great-granddaughter Irene Bjerky.

each. Their movements made the early newspapers throughout the province as citizens and storekeepers anticipated their arrival.

Sperry "Dutch" Cline was the provincial constable in Hazelton in the early 1900s. Cline described Cataline as "a striking figure with a Buffalo Bill head of hair and a Napoleon III imperial beard—broad-shouldered, barrel-chested and tapered from the waist to the narrow hips and thin shanks of men who spend a lifetime on horseback. His already commanding presence was further enhanced by his apparel, which seldom varied: a broad-brimmed sombrero, a silk handkerchief around his neck, a frock coat, heavy woollen trousers and a rather dainty pair of riding boots."

Wes Jasper was part of an experimental cattle drive in 1910 that brought cattle from the Chilcotin to Hazelton. Jasper encountered Cataline in Quesnel with an incredibly large sixty-horse and sixty-mule pack train. He kindly offered Jasper advice on places to overnight the cattle where there would be enough feed for the animals.

Cataline was reportedly helpful to the local First Nations people, handing out provisions when he felt they were needed and not asking for repayment. Unlike some of the other operators, Cataline never had animals go missing at night. He soon became a renowned pack-train operator, with a firm hand and a very strong team.

Cataline met an aboriginal woman named Mary in Wrangell, Alaska, early in his life; they married in 1876. Together they had a daughter named Clemence. Cataline later married Amelia York of Spuzzum and had two or three children with her. He may not have seen much of his children, but records show he kept in contact. Amelia regularly received gold eagle coins from him.

With an amazing memory, Cataline always knew where supplies were going, how much was owed to him for his goods, and how much he owed his own employees. Keeping no written ledgers, he was able to retain and recite everything from memory.

Portrait of Jean Caux (Cataline). Photo from Yale Museum courtesy of Irene Bjerky.

When settling up with an employee, Cataline once said, "Six dollars cash to Soda Creek; two dollars 100 Mile House; three dollars Clinton; five dollars Lac La Hache; two dollars Bonaparte Reserve; three dollars Ashcroft; fifty cents 150 Mile House for tobacco; two dollars Hazelton for whiskey; five dollars Hazelton pay fine." After doing the calculations in his head, he had a store agent write a cheque and let the packer go.

Cataline managed very large quantities of gear and reportedly every item ordered arrived at its destination, except one incident when one of his packers

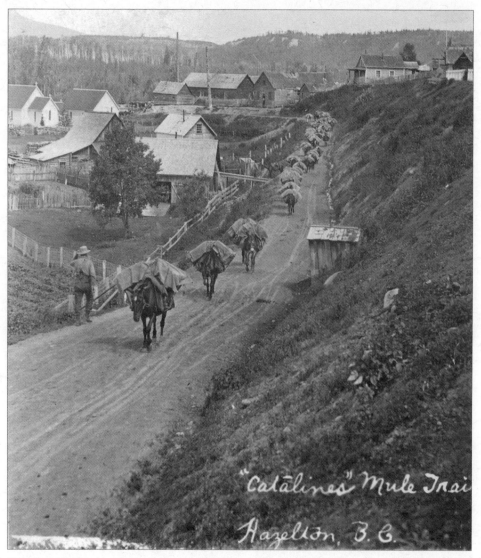

"Cataline's" Mule Trail
Hazelton B.C.

One of Cataline's pack trains heads up the hill and out of Hazelton, bound for remote destinations to the north and east. Photo courtesy of Bulkley Valley Museum, P0336.

mistakenly threw out two pounds of Limburger cheese, thinking the package contained something rotten. Cataline learned of the mistake and promptly ordered a replacement cheese.

At one point Cataline lost some of his pack animals to disease and went to a bank for a loan to purchase replacements. Upon hearing how many horses and mules he owned, the bank granted him the loan. At the end of the season, when Cataline returned to repay the loan, the manager observed that he had a significant amount of money on him and suggested he put it in the bank. But when Cataline learned the bank owned no mules or horses, he decided the money was best kept with him and his team.

He was always willing to travel to new mineral claims and remote settlements. Never refusing the needs of a customer, he once transported a steam boiler cut into pieces and strapped on the mules' backs and, amazingly, a piano balanced on a mule with props on each side. The mules were well trained and reportedly went to stand beside their packs when a bell was rung. His employees, on the other hand, may have not been so well behaved: Cataline is said to have carried a mule shoe in his jacket to break up disputes among his crew.

The horseshoe was not his only weapon. He kept a long Mexican knife in one of his tall boots and once stopped a riot from erupting between Judge Begbie and some angry miners. The miners were about to rebel against Judge Begbie when Cataline's pack train arrived. When asked which side he was on, Cataline drew his long knife out of his tall boot and announced, "I stands by judge!" The angry miners sized up Cataline and his husky packers and decided to let the disagreement lie.

The judge did not forget this favour. Years later, Cataline's claim to his land was challenged because he was not a Canadian citizen. Judge Begbie went out and declared Cataline a Canadian citizen in an impromptu court session on the dusty Cariboo road. When the land issue was called to Judge Begbie's court he declared, "Why, I myself declared Cataline a Canadian citizen. Next case!"

Cataline retired in 1913, at age eighty-three. He sold his pack train operation to George Beirnes of the Kispiox Valley and settled down in a small cabin Beirnes gave him on Mission Point, across the Bulkley River from Hazelton.

Cataline was a tough man who spent most of his life outside. He encountered many days of inclement weather while riding over difficult terrain, cooking over a fire and sleeping on a canvas pack-cover under the stars.

Even in his late retirement he showed he was made of tough stuff. He reportedly never wore socks, even in the coldest of winters. Cline, Cataline's friend from Hazelton, recalls one especially cold and icy January when Cataline came into the Hudson's Bay Store and asked for one pair of thick wool socks. Heads turned and the locals wondered if old Cataline was finally feeling the cold. But before leaving the store he pulled his new socks over his leather boots—for sure footing on the slippery ice.

When his health began to fail, Cataline refused to go to the hospital. His friends once carried him out of his house and loaded him on a wagon destined for the hospital, only to see him revive in the fresh air, roll out of the wagon and return to his cabin.

In the autumn of 1922, at the age of ninety-two, Cataline died and was buried in the Gitanmaax Cemetery in Hazelton. The memorial cairn there now was established by the citizens of Hazelton after they could not locate his grave. His descendants returned to the cemetery in 2009 and mounted a brass plaque on the cairn for Cataline, the indomitable packer.

STERNWHEELERS ON THE SKEENA

The mighty Skeena River flows past the historic community of Hazelton and drops a remarkable eight hundred feet over almost two hundred miles to join the ocean at Prince Rupert. Despite the river's sharp curves, rocky canyons and temperamental water levels, it was once a major transportation route for First Nations people, explorers and early settlers.

In the early years of white exploration and settlement, impressive canoe brigades moved up and down the Skeena, bringing supplies from the Hudson's Bay post at coastal Port Simpson to the inland post at Hazelton. It took about one week for four or five strong First Nations men in a fully loaded canoe to battle the current upriver to Hazelton. They used a combination of poles, oars and ropes to pull and push their way upstream. These experienced river-men would unload the Hudson's Bay Company supplies, then load the canoes with large bundles of furs and the occasional passenger—and return to Port Essington in just over one day.

In 1864 and 1866 two sternwheelers for the Collins Overland Telegraph Company attempted to go up the Skeena, but both underestimated the strong current and moody disposition of the water. Neither sternwheeler succeeded in churning past the Kitsumkalum River, in the vicinity of today's Terrace.

For many years the Hudson's Bay Company (HBC) relied on canoes and river-wise First Nations men to bring freight upriver. In 1890, the company took a chance and built the *Caledonia*—the first riverboat for the Skeena River. The

Two sternwheelers taking on wood at Kitsumkalum near present-day Terrace. Photo courtesy of Bulkley Valley Museum, P0555.

First Nations canoes travelled the river from the coast into the interior long before wood-powered paddlewheelers took up the job. Photo courtesy of Telkwa Museum, P0160.

mighty Skeena discouraged the boat's first two captains, but the third, J.H. Bonser, was up to the challenge.

Art Downs, in his book *Paddlewheelers on the Frontier*, states that it was Captain Bonser who named many of the rougher spots along the Skeena, like the Hornet's Nest, the Whirly Gig and Devil's Elbow. Downs writes that for years the *Caledonia* was the only sternwheeler on the river. Bonser learned where landlines had to be secured to large ringbolts on rocky islands, where on the riverbank to keep a supply of wood and, most importantly, exactly how many inches of water the paddles required to make it over submerged rocks.

Competition for the *Caledonia* was inevitable, though, and arrived in 1901 with the construction and launch of the sternwheeler *Hazelton*. Robert Cunningham had the *Hazelton* built to ensure that supplies for his store in the village of Hazelton would no longer be subject to the whims of a Hudson's Bay Company boat. Cunningham guaranteed a rivalry by not only asking the HBC's Bonser to help design the new paddleboat, but also managed to convince him to quit the HBC to pilot the *Hazelton*.

In response to Cunningham's bold move, and the loss of Captain Bonser, the HBC built yet another sternwheeler, the *Mount Royal*. Constructed of Douglas fir and eastern oak, the new boat had luxurious quarters built to pamper passengers. However, during her launch in April 1902, the lavish *Mount Royal* became tangled in her ropes, and several days of struggle followed before the vessel was successfully launched into the water. A bad launch is considered an ill omen, and in this case it was one that came to be fulfilled.

The HBC's *Mount Royal*, under its new commander, Captain Johnson, and the *Hazelton*, with veteran Captain Bonser, quickly developed an intense rivalry. The sternwheelers stole each other's woodpiles and dangerously crowded each other in the strong river currents.

Passengers joined the chaos, jeering at the other boat and cheering on their own captains. The paddleboats sought to make the fastest round-trip from Port Essington to Hazelton and back; beating the other's time was paramount. Passengers and riverside settlers encouraged the competition by wagering on record-breaking times, first spring run upriver, or last boat before winter.

The first boat of the season to reach Hazelton was celebrated, and in the spring of 1904 Bonser on the *Hazelton* and Captain Johnson on the *Mount Royal* vied for the honour. Longtime Skeena River explorer Wiggs O'Neill recalls the rivalry in the "Battle of Hardscrabble Rapids." O'Neill records that the *Hazelton* left the coast first, but stopped for wood at Hardscrabble Rapids, near present-day Usk. While there, the *Mount Royal* gained on them. Wood and men were rushed aboard and the *Hazelton* pulled out just as the *Mount Royal* approached. Much to the delight of the passengers, the two sternwheelers raced bow to bow. The *Mount Royal* crowded the *Hazelton* into shallow water and slowly began to pull ahead. But Captain Bonser would not allow the loss, and recklessly rammed the *Mount Royal*. Captain Johnson lost control of his boat, which was carried downstream bow first. Downs writes in *Paddlewheelers on the Frontier* that Captain Bonser wagged the *Hazelton*'s stern and tooted the whistle as they continued upstream. In a rage suited to the Wild West, Captain Johnson rushed out of the *Mount Royal*'s pilothouse and fired a rifle at the departing *Hazelton*.

The battle at Hardscrabble Rapids ended up in Marine Court. Johnson claimed his boat was deliberately rammed by Bonser, and Bonser insisted it was an accident. Both men were reprimanded—Bonser for ramming another vessel, Johnson for leaving his helm—and the case was closed.

At the time of the settlement, Robert Cunningham was moving his freight on the *Hazelton* at a loss, and the HBC believed the competition between the sternwheelers was cutting into their bottom line. They offered to purchase the *Hazelton* from Cunningham, guaranteeing as well to move all his freight for free. Cunningham accepted, and the HBC took the *Hazelton* out of service, putting their former captain out of a job. Bonser went south to work on the Fraser River, while Captain Johnson and the *Mount Royal* continued freighting on the Skeena.

In the summer of 1907, on a return trip downriver from Hazelton, the fate from its bad launch caught up with the *Mount Royal*. As Johnson piloted the vessel into the raging waters of Kitselas Canyon, a strong wind pushed it onto an island of rocks, impaling the bow. With the boat stuck, Johnson ordered a gangplank be placed across to the rocky island. Twenty-some passengers were safely evacuated, most not realizing the danger they were in, and some even reluctant to leave their plush quarters for a stormy rock.

Captain Johnson had just stepped ashore and intended to return to help his crewmen moor the *Mount Royal* to a tree when the boat suddenly turned, splintering her paddlewheel against the opposite bank. Wedged across the canyon like a dam, the violent current quickly turned the *Mount Royal* bottom up and hurtled her through the canyon. Six men died in the upheaval.

It took many hours for the people of nearby Kitselas to rescue the passengers from the rocky island. Bales of furs were found downstream and stretched out to dry. It is rumoured that the *Mount Royal*'s safe, supposedly containing the gold of the prospectors leaving Hazelton, still lies at the bottom of the canyon.

The HBC built a replacement vessel, the *Port Simpson*, and in 1908 Captain Johnson returned to the helm. This was the beginning of the railway-building boom and many more sternwheelers took to the Skeena. Some were owned by the Grand Trunk Pacific Railway for transporting their men and materials, some

The *Hazelton*, one of the first sternwheelers to ply the Skeena River. Photo courtesy of Bulkley Valley Museum, P0147

by railway subcontractors Foley, Welch and Stewart, and one was owned by Pat Burns, for supplying meat to the camps and settlements.

Captain Johnson was lured away from the HBC to work with the railway, organizing its fleet of sternwheelers that supplied their construction camps. Captain Bonser returned to the Skeena to pilot the *Inlander*, a vessel owned by merchants at Kitselas and Hazelton.

In 1912 the railway bridge over the Skeena was completed and there was no longer a need for sternwheelers to move freight and passengers on the river. That fall, the last sternwheeler—the *Inlander*—left Hazelton and paddled down the Skeena, captained by pioneer Captain Bonser.

Large ringbolts remain attached to rocky walls and islands as testament to the sternwheeler captains and the First Nations men poling and paddling their way up and down the historic Skeena River route.

A GREAT CATCH—THE SKEENA SALMON-CANNING INDUSTRY

Towards the end of the 1870s, anticipating the inevitable end of the gold rush, northern businessmen looked around for their next "gold" resource. With the potential market for canned salmon abroad, they invested in Skeena River salmon. Early explorers, anthropologists, miners and settlers had all noted the abundance of the Skeena's salmon as well as the advanced technologies and knowledge the coastal and interior First Nations people had developed for their capture, processing and storage. Canneries were built along the river to catch, can and export the salmon that gathered at the estuary and swam upstream.

The Skeena's salmon runs include coho, pink, chum, spring and sockeye. The sockeye's silver markings and bright pink flesh were a marketing dream; the canning labels prominently displayed a leaping silver fish and the words "Skeena River." In this way the northern canneries distinguished themselves as unique from those in the south, and the Skeena gained a reputation for producing salmon that were superior to those of the Fraser.

The Inverness cannery was built in 1876 and was quickly followed by the Aberdeen, North Pacific, Carlisle, Claxton and Port Essington canneries. Joan Skogan, in her book *Skeena, A River Remembered*, wrote, "... by 1902 fourteen

The cannery buildings are visible in the background. Net mending was a large job, sometimes fulfilled by skilled First Nations women. Photo courtesy of Prince Rupert City and Regional Archives, JD Allen Fonds, P991.56.5893.

canneries are scattered along the Skeena, from Standard Point off the river mouth to Aberdeen fifteen miles upriver from Sockeye Point on the slough.... Clusters of wooden buildings united by boardwalks and docks dotted the estuary from Porcher and Smith Island off the Skeena's entrance to Aberdeen fifteen miles upriver." These canneries gave rise to small towns, with seasonal populations to support stores, doctors, and even a Salvation Army brass marching band. Skogan notes that canneries were quick to claim sites on the river mouth: "They built canneries as close as possible to the home-coming salmon and the labour force who traveled the river to reach the plants."

Although the salmon-canning season didn't start until June, there were months of preparation. Alfred Carmichael worked at the Aberdeen Windsor Cannery in 1891 and his reminiscences were printed in a 1970 *Skeena Digest*. Carmichael recalled that, "during the winter while in Victoria, the cannery manager makes a contract with a Chinese firm to do the following: first, make the cans, and second, handle the salmon, which includes cleaning, filling of cans, soldering, testing, boiling,

The fishing boats that worked the mouth of the Skeena in the early years of the salmon-canning industry were open and non-motorized. This boat has just unloaded its haul at the cannery dock. Photo courtesy of Prince Rupert City and Regional Archives and Museum of Northern BC, Wrathall Collection, WP996.71.11090.

putting on labels and casing. The tools are supplied by the company. When fishing commences, the Chinese-boss hires Indians to clean the fish and to fill the cans."

First Nations women and men, and in some cases even their children, found employment at the canneries. The upriver First Nations came down the Skeena by canoe and, after the Grand Trunk Pacific Railway was built, by train. They were employed to catch and clean fish and to fill cans. Noted for their skills, First Nations women were hired to make new nets and mend old ones.

The fishing season started out on the ocean for three weeks as the salmon returned, then the fish were followed as they moved into the estuary and up the Skeena River. To man the rowboats and handle the nets, the canneries employed hundreds of men who had the brute strength to manage the tides and haul in nets heavily laden with fish.

Gillnet fishermen's boats were towed to the fishing grounds by steam tugboats. Walter Wicks wrote, in *Pioneer Days of British Columbia*, Volume Two, that the twenty-six-foot boats were open—they had no cabin for shelter and were propelled only by a strong back, ten-foot-long oars and a sail. Each cannery painted its boats a different colour; some had flags displaying the cannery's name. The gillnetters were left on the fishing grounds, two to a boat. Wicks wrote that one man worked at casting the net over the stern while the other rowed until the full thousand feet of net was laid out on the water. The men drifted all night, then hauled in the nets in the morning. Wicks wrote that, "the man rowing would back the boat toward the net while his partner hauled it in."

When fishing on the Skeena, Wicks and other fishermen had to contend with sandbars, reefs, sunken logs and tides. Canneries sent out so many fishermen that nets tangled, boats were stuck on sandbars, and curses were exchanged in Japanese, Chinese, English and various First Nations languages.

As for the value of the fish, Alfred Carmichael, working at the Inverness cannery in 1891, wrote "This year 25 cents was paid for a spring salmon and 6 cents for a sockeye, not considering the weight. For instance, a spring weighing 10 pounds would fetch the same as one 80 pounds in weight. I remember a spring was caught weighing 78 pounds but no more than 25 cents was allowed for it."

In an effort to allow a healthy number of salmon to escape the nets, the Fisheries Department enforced a 6:00 am to 6:00 pm Sunday closure. Wicks recalled that this was the day men found a washbasin, repaired their boats, mended nets, and readied themselves for the next week.

Carmichael explained that workers at the early canneries worked in assembly-line style to produce as many cans as possible. First the heads, tails and guts of the fish were removed and dumped into the river, then the cans were packed full and soldered shut. The cans rolled down a chute to the bath room before being cooled and stacked. This was not an automated system; hundreds of men and women (and some children) worked to fulfill each of these tasks.

Records show that the salmon catch, although abundant, was unpredictable. In 1877, the Inverness cannery—the first on the Skeena—packed three thousand

Pioneer Women

Pioneer women who moved into and settled this area were witness to incredible growth in a short period of time—from horse and buggies along the First Nations trails to the sternwheeler era to the railway completion and the first vehicles in the area. They adapted to change, endured hardships and overcame day-to-day challenges in a new environment. These women helped establish our communities, our schools, hospitals and halls. "Too often," wrote Lillian Weedmark, past curator of the Bulkley Valley Museum in Smithers, BC, "we give credit only to people we recognize as being supremely accomplished, failing to recognize that often what might seem ordinary is not. Pioneer women were not ordinary."

The women who came here or were born here lived in an isolated and often challenging landscape. Mattie Frank is an example. Her story is recorded in a 1967 Women's Institute publication, *Pioneer Women*. The text states that Mattie was born in Norway and married Henry Frank at Port Essington at the mouth of the Skeena River in 1900. She had four children and moved to Kitsumkalum in 1908, where she assisted in the start-up of Frank Brothers Dairy. Her fifth child was born there and later two more children. "Her first home was a tent, then a log cabin, and later a large log house. Winters were isolated and mail came by dogsled. They shopped every six months in Port Essington," this publication states.

The life of a pioneer woman was busy with chores. Women had soap to make, butter to churn, cows to milk. Often wives and mothers were left alone to tend the house, farm and children while their husbands went away for long periods to work. In the early days, many of the farmers relied upon the winter work of cutting and hauling railway ties, which took them away from their homes for weeks at a time.

Nan Bourgon wrote that in those days most of the money went into the farms and the women had to "make do." Pioneer woman Fay Ball of the Topley and Forestdale Women's Institute wrote, "I made my own yarn from sheep's wool. All the children's clothes were hand me downs or made over." Another woman recalls using flour sacking to sew clothes for her children. Nan Bourgon in *Pioneer Women* reflects upon the women who settled the area and eloquently summarizes, "I am amazed, not so much at what she did as what she did without."

The women worked hard and relied upon themselves and each other to survive difficult situations.

In a new northern landscape, they started families and found themselves in a rural life that was challenging and in some cases very isolated. Women sought out each other for an organized support system. The women met in churches, neighbourhood halls and kitchens. New settlers enjoyed spending time with the pioneer women, who often shared advice on childcare, medicine, food production and farm and household maintenance. Women who had any nursing experience were relied upon for medical advice; they became midwives for their neighbours, pulled teeth and even conducted surgery on horses and livestock. There were extremes of weather to cope with, and drought, floods and fires.

Smithers and Driftwood pioneer Mrs. Lapadat wrote in *Pioneer Women* that "many hardships were encountered and overcome through the many years of pioneering. At the time there was so much happiness and gaiety in the life of the pioneer women, as well as a sense of achievement." The women and their Women's Institutes celebrated. They organized social events, fundraisers and initiated community-minded campaigns. The same women advocated for social change. They purchased materials and supported the construction of schools, community halls and churches. For example, the women's institute in Rose Lake was instrumental in bringing the telephone service to the area. And the various northern branches of the Women's Institute all assisted in getting consistent medical care in the north.

Fundraising events, Christmas concerts, pageants and dances were organized by the women to form community connections. Some taught in the pioneer schoolhouses; others ran the rural post offices. This was the first generation of women to wear the pants, literally. Palling pioneer Lydia Saunders recalls in *Pioneer Women* that she rode horseback to Ootsa Lake in 1913 and "was not too prudish to wear overalls, in contrast to her mother's hardship four years earlier over the Bella Coola trail in the modest long skirts of the day."

Too often pioneer women are identified vaguely as "Mrs." or "the wife of" and often are not mentioned at all until there is a child born. We owe a special debt of gratitude to these women, often unnamed and hidden in the history books, who helped settle this country and endured hardships with a positive spirit to build our schools, halls, churches and our communities.

Skeena River Salmon Fisheries
Part of the Pack   AllenPhoto

More than one hundred thousand tins of canned salmon await shipment at a cannery on the Skeena.
Photo courtesy of Prince Rupert City and Regional Archives, JD Allen Fonds, P991.56.5893.

48-pound cases. Skogan shows the annual variations clearly: "In 1905, twelve Skeena plants canned 114,085 cases; in 1922 thirteen plants recorded 482,305 cases. The five canneries remaining in 1956 put up only 55,527 cases. In 1981... Port Edward and Cassiar produced over 300,000 cases."

Successful canneries were those that could outlast the inevitable bad years until the next plentiful run. After the 1920s, the number of operating Skeena canneries steadily decreased. Skogan points out that bad seasons and boundary changes took their toll, sending some canneries into closure. Some suffered from fires that spread rapidly through their wooden buildings. Cassiar, built in 1903, outlasted all the others, operating until 1983.

Cannery owners and workers of the past carried on in spite of setbacks and adversity. Like those fishing the Skeena today, the canneries were endlessly optimistic that the next season would prove to be better and bigger than the last.

REVEREND FRED STEPHENSON

When the Bulkley Valley's Mel Coulson marvels at the early pioneers' strength of conviction, he is thinking of one man in particular: the Reverend Fred Stephenson. "He seemed to be inured to cold, capable of immense physical exertion, and able to exist on the most meagre food rations."

Coulson should know; he spent many months researching the life of Reverend Stephenson. What began as a small project, researching the history of the Anglican Church in northern BC for his fellow Anglican parishioners, resulted in a vast amount of material and lots of anecdotes about Stephenson's life.

Fred L. Stephenson came to Victoria from England in 1884. He was ordained into the Anglican Church in 1889 and the same year married Emily Fisher. The newlyweds took a small, three-masted steamer up the BC coast and lived and worked among the Coast Tsimshian in Kitkatla. Emily gave birth to their first daughter in 1891 but they lost her to whooping cough that spread through the village. Four more children were born to them in Kitkatla, followed later by two more as the family moved around northern BC.

In 1898, Stephenson was dispatched to Bennett Lake to minister to the thousands of gold seekers pouring over the Chilkoot Pass to seek their fortunes in the Klondike gold fields.

In 1899 Stephenson walked into the pioneer gold-mining town of Atlin. He preached throughout the town wherever he could. It was in Atlin that he earned his nickname, "the fighting parson." Allison Mitcham, in her book *The Last Utopia: Atlin*, writes that the reverend was being harassed by a rough miner who told Stephenson, and the crowd gathered around them, that if Stephenson hadn't been a man of the cloth he would whip him. To which Reverend Stephenson threw his coat on the ground and said, "There lies the cloth, here stands the man. Come to him." Coulson continues the story: "Shocked out of his bullying stance and regaining some measure of sobriety, the miner backed down and offered Stephenson his hand." Such a fighting stance gained respect and reputation in the rough-and-tumble northern community.

Telkwa's St. Stephens Anglican Church, built in 1910 by Reverend Stephenson and his fundraising work. This was the second Anglican church that he helped construct; the first was St. Martin's in Atlin in 1910. Photo courtesy of Telkwa Museum.

After several years in Atlin, and walking many hundreds of miles to preach to surrounding camps and communities, the reverend was offered a three-month holiday by his bishop. He could go south for a break, or he could attempt a hike, in winter, through mountain ranges known to be inhospitable even in the best summer months, along the telegraph line and onwards to Kuldo, Kispiox, Hazelton and eventually to Aldermere in the Bulkley Valley. Stephenson wrote, "my friends tried to dissuade me from it. But as I had suggested the trip to my bishop and he had taken me up and called my bluff I either had to make good or stand down." He decided he had to take the "holiday" and do the trek from Atlin to Aldermere.

As winter arrived in 1905, the reverend began training to get himself fit for the trip. "Every day I did not less than 10 miles tramping or snowshoeing over the worst country I could pick, deliberately choosing places where difficulties were bound to be met." The men living in isolated cabins along the telegraph line heard of his plan to hike the route and sent him encouragement over the wire; they were lonely for company and looked forward to a guest.

January 1906 arrived, and with it, heavy snowfalls. Reverend Stephenson wrote that on March 3, 1906, he "... hooked up the dogs, waved goodbye to those who stood on the wharf of [Atlin Lake] to see me start and began the first lap of my long-talked-of trip." A three-dog team was used to haul a sled and pack the gear. Stephenson valued his dogs and knew that their strength had to be conserved or they would never endure the months of daily work ahead, so he packed the snow ahead of them. "I broke the trail for half a mile stretch and then returned over my tracks to pound the snow more solidly before I put the dogs to work to haul the loaded sleigh that far," he wrote. He knew that "unless the trail was broken for them we would make less distance in the day's run and the dogs would be more fatigued."

The reverend slept in linemen's cabins or the "refuge cabins" between them, or he covered himself with canvas and bedded down with his dogs. He crossed treacherous ice, broke his snowshoes, built temporary bridges and used ropes to lower dogs, gear and himself down steep slopes. After leaving the telegraph trail and breaking out on his own path, he ran out of food but was lucky to come upon a trapper who welcomed him to a feast of lynx stew. Forced to abandon his sled at the Nass Summit, the dogs carried on with forty-pound packs. In fitting biblical language, Stephenson called the entrance to the pass "the Jaws of Death," the other end "the Gates of Hell." He crossed the Nass River and walked to Kuldo and Kispiox. After forty-six days of steady slogging, he met his brother on the trail outside Hazelton. So travel-worn and emaciated was the reverend that his own brother didn't recognize him.

In May 1906, Stephenson pitched a tent at Tyhee Lake. The Walking Parson meant to return to Atlin but was asked by the bishop to stay on in the Bulkley Valley. He made his home in Aldermere (near present-day Telkwa), and built a mission room to live in and work from. His wife and children came from Metchosin to join him at Aldermere, and another child was born.

Reverend Stephenson's work was not confined to the Bulkley Valley. Settlers had begun to move to Pleasant Valley (now Houston), North and South Bulkley, Burns Lake, François Lake and Ootsa Lake. Every winter, Stephenson strapped a seventy-five-pound pack on his back and set off on a journey of two to three hundred miles. He writes, "Many a time I thought the only difference between me and a mule was the length of my ears." He preached in whatever covered space was available; people sat on overturned apple crates and barrels. If a stranger had happened by and glanced in through a window, they wouldn't have been able to tell the reverend from the common folk. The settlers referred to him as a sky pilot, meaning he had a direct line to the heavens.

Reverend Stephenson stayed in the Bulkley Valley until 1913 when he followed his wife and children to Victoria. He was appointed rector to Ladysmith until 1914 when he, along with his two oldest sons, enlisted in the Canadian armed forces. He served as chaplain with the 49th (Edmonton) Battalion. He was wounded and gassed, and convalesced at Shaughnessy Military Hospital. He returned to minister at Cowichan and Victoria before retiring in 1927. He died in 1941 at age seventy-seven.

"The people that lived before us seem a different breed altogether," concludes Coulson. "They were tough and resourceful; somehow we have gotten soft since that time." Fred Stephenson certainly epitomizes Coulson's idea of the pioneering spirit.

THE TELKWA BARBECUE

In 1912, Telkwa had a thriving little main street beside the Bulkley River. Situated on a ridge above Telkwa, the community of Aldermere had a prosperous hotel, the *Interior News* and a busy wagon road. Smithers was not yet even named on a map let alone staked on the ground.

The people of Aldermere and Telkwa were pioneers to the landscape; each person brought with them memories of their last homes where annual fairs or exhibitions were the mark of a successful, permanent community. Fairs were a way of showing your personal best in growing crops and raising livestock. Fairs showed off your community. Horse races, livestock sales and rodeos often occurred in conjunction with a community fair.

As early as 1910, the residents of Telkwa and Aldermere were rustling up support for a fair. In 1910, the *Interior News* stated, "... here would be seen the biggest and best of everything the country produces; people from every quarter would meet and swap ideas, horses and other things." Two years later, in 1912, members of the newly formed Bulkley Valley Agricultural Association met and discussed hosting an exhibition, a barbecue and a rodeo in Telkwa. Perhaps they met in Telkwa on Riverside Street, hitching their horses outside Mason Adams' Drug Store and sitting on tall stools inside to discuss hosting an event that was sure to draw wagonloads of people to their small village.

Led by Telkwa bookkeeper Tom Thorp, the elected association members took hats off their heads and went around Telkwa and surrounding areas collecting money and generating interest in a local fair, with horse races and a beef barbecue, to be held in the third week of September, 1912. An ad was placed in the *Interior News* looking for entries. Some locals scoffed at their ambition; surely a fair could not be pulled off successfully with less than two months to organize it. But the organizers were encouraged by people's interest and optimistically referred to the event as the first annual fair.

Volunteer work crews built benches against a hill and laid out a horse-racing track on what was at that time an empty, open space near Telkwa's newly constructed Roman Catholic Church. Spots were designated for exhibit tents. The barbecue pit was dug and lined with rocks. Programs were printed and categories for grain, horses, stock and vegetables were established and posted. Judges were chosen. It was a sign of the times that First Nations men had a separate category in the horse events: "Indian Horse Race, ½ mile." There were also "a number of competitions interesting to housewives."

Government representatives travelled to Telkwa for the occasion. There were wagon roads through the valley at this time, both the high road to Aldermere and another across the Bulkley River with bridges crossing both the Telkwa and the Bulkley Rivers to reach the Telkwa townsite. The Grand Trunk Pacific Railway had just laid tracks through Telkwa and passenger service was available. Hundreds of people came to Telkwa from all around the Northwest, and the first annual Bulkley Valley Agricultural Exhibition was held in Telkwa, Saturday, September 21, 1912.

Exhibit tents filled up with eggs, butter, bread, jam and flowers. This first fair had no gates or turnstiles; instead the fair organizers sold royal blue souvenir ribbons and everyone attending the fair and barbecue purchased one. A mineral tent showing mineral samples from the nearby mining claims drew a large crowd. The vegetable exhibit received a special mention in the next issue of the *Interior News*: "... giant cabbages, titanic turnips and enormous potatoes amazing the beholder."

Cooked beef is removed from the barbecue pit at one of the early Telkwa Barbecues. Today, nearly one hundred years later, the beef is still cooked the same way. Photo courtesy of Telkwa Museum, P0109.

At a display of grains, entries of timothy hay, oats, barley and wheat crowded the tent space. Cattle and horses were in the centre ring with races and competitions occurring throughout the day. This first fair also featured a "refreshment" tent located incongruously beside the rifle gallery, yet the day went off without a hitch.

A newspaper editorial following the fair read, "To an old-timer it was the beginning of the 'at last,' the dawn of prosperity for which we had so patiently waited. To the new-comer it was the triumphant vindication of his choice of abode and to the world at large it showed clearly that, after many years of pioneer work, a new country was ready for both miner and agriculturalist."

The annual fall fair continued in Telkwa and became known as the Telkwa Barbecue because of the popularity of the pit-roasted beef lunch. Newspaper ads boasted, "If you go hungry—blame yourself. Not us." In 1914 a quarter-mile

Early versions of the annual Telkwa Barbecue included horse races and, starting in 1914, rodeo events. Photo courtesy of Telkwa Museum, P0264.

race track was in use, and the event featured a rodeo that advertised "thrills and spills." By 1916, according to the *Interior News*, "horse racing was the principal amusement of the day" and large crowds of people attended "by train and motor." Posters for the Telkwa Barbecue in 1918 promised an auction of a rail-car load of two-year-old heifers, and "at noon a steer will be roasting over the pit. This work will be in the charge of Nels White who all of you know to be the best at this kind of thing in British Columbia. Nuff said."

The 1918 barbecue also added pillow fights to the program. The railway offered special rates to those passengers attending the barbecue. In 1919 the exhibitions were moved to Smithers and their "Fall Fair," the Bulkley Valley Exhibition, was held in September. Also in 1919, the site of the Telkwa Barbecue was designated by the provincial government for a new Telkwa school and the Telkwa Barbecue

Aldermere's Telkwa Hotel

The Telkwa Hotel in Aldermere figures large in the early stories and memoirs of the pioneer town. The hotel was a frequent stopping place for road-weary travellers on their way through the Bulkley Valley. Aldermere was staked in 1901 and a few years later the settlement had its first hotel built by Lem Broughton, a telegraph operator, and Jack MacNeil, an entrepreneur. Sperry "Dutch" Cline visited Aldermere's Telkwa Hotel and writes in *Pioneer Days In British Columbia* that "the builders had exhausted the supply of whipsawn lumber and large portions of the floor were lacking." A single cottonwood plank was the large bar and only four feet of floor, just in front of the bar, was laid. Cline writes, "This platform provided solid footing for a patron when hoisting a drink, while the unfloored portion served to prove a guest's condition when leaving the bar." If they made it along the narrow plank from the bar to the door they were considered sober, but "if they fell off they might be considered impaired." The second floor, the sleeping quarters, also had significant gaps in the flooring. One night when Cline left his stool at the bar and was making his way across the planks on the second floor to his bed, he was the victim of a prank. Someone had rearranged the floorboards and Cline fell through to the first floor: "I landed at the very spot I had vacated a few minutes before." Cline says he felt a pain in his leg, but "dared not admit it because anything short of a compound fracture would have added to the hilarity of the crowd."

Aldermere was a busy centre with heavily laden wagons pulled by four- and six-horse teams stopping for the night in the Telkwa Hotel or one of the other rooming

The Telkwa Hotel in Aldermere, BC, located on the bench above Telkwa along the busy wagon road. Photo courtesy of Bulkley Valley Museum, P0227.

houses and taking advantage of the running water piped up the hill from the Bulkley River as well as the newspaper, the laundry, the blacksmith and livery stables. The hotel was improved and expanded, and it became a meeting place and was used by Reverend Stephenson for services before he built St. Stephen's Anglican Church in Telkwa. By 1913, the community of Aldermere was declining in population and the stores, including the hotel, were moving down the hill to the riverside community of Telkwa. No trace of Aldermere remains today, only a walking trail that citizens of Telkwa and bears frequent. Standing among the overgrown aspens are a few interpretive plaques with photographs of early Aldermere.

committee had to find a new site. The committee officers were determined to keep hosting an annual event and secured land across the Bulkley where they have proudly continued their barbecue tradition every autumn.

The original site of the Telkwa Barbecue is now the Telkwa Elementary School's field. The rock-lined barbecue pit is grassed over and its whereabouts unknown. The bluffs where the crowds perched to watch the horse races is now a favourite winter sledding hill for the locals. The Roman Catholic Church that once stood alone in the background of photographs has been converted into a busy daycare. The wide open space where horses once raced and jumped hurdles is now fenced yards, homes and residential streets.

The Bulkley Valley Kinsmen have organized the annual event since the mid-1960s. In 1981, when the horse races and rodeo were not drawing the crowds they needed, a demolition derby was added to the program. The barbecue continued on its new site and celebrated its 100th anniversary in 2012. The local Kinsmen worked very hard to see an impressive outdoor timber-framed stage built on the barbecue grounds. The 100th barbecue was celebrated in style with a large demolition derby and two concerts on the new stage surrounded by sold-out crowds. The local Kinsmen are excited about continuing the legacy of the Telkwa Barbecue. They have similar bold ambitions to those who started the annual Telkwa event and, judging from history, the Telkwa Barbecue will continue for many more years.

JOSEPH COYLE—EGG SAFETY CARTON INVENTOR

J oseph Coyle worked in a newspaper office in Juneau, Alaska, before moving to Hazelton in 1908. Coyle had worked in a newspaper office as a teenager in Ontario and later worked at a printing press as a typesetter. When Coyle arrived in Hazelton, he found the community was full of local news and regional rumours yet there was no newspaper. Coyle possessed keen business sense and in July 1908, he founded the *Omenica Herald* in Hazelton.

Coyle wasn't in Hazelton for long before he moved his family and his printing press to Aldermere, near present-day Telkwa, and started the *Interior News* in 1909. Coyle made friends with the nearby telegraph operator, "Spud" Murphy. Spud passed along the news of the world, with a side of local tidbits, to the newspaper man in Aldermere. The local coming and going of folks was reported right alongside the world news. Joseph Coyle and his wife had a daughter, Ellen, who was one of the few children in Aldermere at that time.

As a newspaper man, Coyle made it his business to know everyone else's. Coyle learned of an ongoing dispute between a hotel in Aldermere and a local farmer, Gabriel Lacroix. The hotel blamed the packer for their eggs being cracked upon arrival at their back door kitchen and the packer blamed the hotel owner for breaking

Aldermere's citizenry, the Aldermere Board of Trade. The publisher of the *Interior News*, Joseph Coyle, is in the back row at the far left of the photo, wearing a vest, and his daughter Ellen is seated on the porch in front of him. Photo courtesy of Bulkley Valley Museum, P01480.

Joseph Coyle and Tyhee Lake telegraph operator Mr. Murphy standing in Aldermere, 1911. Photo courtesy of Bulkley Valley Museum, P1488.

the eggs and blaming the transportation. In those days, the eggs were transported either in shallow wooden boxes with small wooden dividers or stacked on top of one another in a wire egg basket. This heated dispute at the hotel over cracked eggs caught Coyle's attention and he set his mind to inventing a solution.

Coyle was no stranger to invention. As a young man in Ontario, he had designed a boat that could be propelled by bicycle pedals, as well as a simple machine for carding wool. He invented a paper egg safety carton that folded up with paper inserts for dividers. The farmer, the packer and the hotel owner were pleased with the results. Coyle produced his egg safety cartons himself for years in Aldermere before moving his family, the *Interior News* and the Coyle Egg Safety Carton business to Smithers in late 1913.

Coyle designed machines to make the egg safety cartons so they became less labour intensive to produce. In 1919, he sold the *Interior News* and his family left

Smithers so he could pursue the life of an inventor in Vancouver. Coyle partnered with United Paper Products to produce the egg safety carton. Investors in the carton were granted licensing rights and the cartons invented by Joseph Coyle in Aldermere, BC, in 1911 were manufactured in London, Ontario, Chicago, New York and Pittsburgh for distribution all around the world. In the 1920s, the New York plant shipped out two hundred million cartons per year. Yet Coyle never profited from the huge success of his invention. He went on to invent a coin sorter, a match dispenser and a fruit box. Later in life, at the age of seventy, Coyle invented another even better egg carton with his son Patrick and set up a business in New Westminster, BC. But their egg carton would be replaced with plastic and moulded egg cartons in the 1970s. Coyle's creative life was long-lived—he died in 1972 at the age of one hundred years.

ROUND LAKE HALL RENEWED

Driving west from Houston, you will eventually come to a high crest in the highway where the valley opens up ahead of you and you can see the Telkwa Range, the Babine Range and, if you're lucky, a first glimpse of the peaks of Hudson Bay Mountain. This area, generally known as Quick, is home to larger acreages, cattle and dairy farms, rambling ranches and homesteads, with residents who know what a calf-puller is and how to plough snow with a tractor.

I lived in Quick at the end of a steep gravel road in a log cabin on a stump farm. The views were stunning and the neighbours made up for their physical distance by being very friendly, dropping by to curse out the encroaching hawk-weed, wonder at the grizzly prints, and help chase cattle back through broken fences. When my husband and I decided to "get hitched," what better spot than the tiny and remote St. John the Divine Anglican Church: quaint and historic, a place where our guests could park by the rural-route mailboxes and walk up a dirt road to the ceremony.

And what better place to have the reception than at the nearby Round Lake Hall, a historic spot—albeit with rustic outhouses and no running water in the kitchen. Our families may have misunderstood what we meant when we said "outdoor plumbing," but not one complained about hiking up the hill behind the hall to the slightly leaning outhouses, or washing their hands with the water jug perched on the stump.

But things have really changed at the hall. It now boasts flush toilets, running water, new windows in all the right places, and all the history of the Quick community.

What is known today as Round Lake Hall was originally the Hubert Hotel, located across the Bulkley River. According to the *Interior News*, the building was purchased by a group of enterprising "farmers' wives" in the winter of 1919 for "socials, dances, card parties, literacy programs, children's entertainment and club meetings." The building was dismantled, then hauled across the frozen Bulkley River and overland to the shores of Round Lake. A community-minded citizen donated land overlooking the lake for the building to sit upon. The women had a site and the materials to start a building, and only needed some money to get the construction started. In 1919 a "fancy dress" fundraiser, called the Rose Ball, was held in Telkwa. The women decorated the hall with five thousand tissue paper roses, the men made pergolas, and attending couples paid five dollars a ticket. The event was popular and raised enough money to start construction of the community building at Round Lake.

Throughout 1920, fifty-four people volunteered and built a simple clubhouse with a fireplace, a large front porch and a grassy area outside for picnics, community games and races. In 1921, the Women's Community Club held the official grand opening. The ceremonies had speeches by club members and provincial politicians, a large picnic, the laying of a cornerstone and a time capsule. Mrs. Ida May Williams spoke at the ceremony and said the hall was "... dedicated to the harmony, contentment and happiness of the district." The advertisement for the opening ceremonies boasted a huge array of activities, including "a Greco Roman wrestling contest, a horse-packing race, chopping contest, tug-of-war (Round Lake vs everyone else), a hurdle race, running high jump, 100-yard dash" and even more. The ad also states, "Water Sports, walking up a greasy pole, tub race, men's swim race" and (and!) "women's and children's contests to be announced on the day of celebration." In case that wasn't enough, the day also featured a Model T race around the lake, which was won by Roy Wakefield. (Some sources say the win was due to the help of a waitress from the Telkwa Hotel weighing down the back end of his car.)

The Round Lake Hall, constructed in the 1920s, became a social centre for the farming community known as Quick. Photo courtesy of Bulkley Valley Museum, P0842.

The hall was historically used for community picnics, and seasonal parties such as Christmas, Hallowe'en and Armistice Day (November 11). During the summer there were swimming, boating and box-lunch socials. Twice a month during the winter horses were hitched up to sleighs and card parties and dances were held at the hall. Local musicians played and people danced into the wee hours, when sleeping children had to be rustled up out of coat piles and loaded onto sleighs for the ride home.

The hall has been heavily used throughout the years and has undergone numerous renovations and repairs. Some locals who were once the children attending the events there insist that the hall has shrunk: they tell me it seemed so much bigger when their mothers and fathers sang and danced there. But, if anything, it has actually expanded over the years.

Since 1958 there has been a steady effort by the Quick community to stabilize and repair the historic building. In 1999, work on the hall's foundation unearthed the time capsule laid by the Women's Community Club in 1921. Inside a glass jar was a note that reads: "Today, July 21st, 1921, this corner stone is laid by the

The hall renovations complete. Photo by Dina Hanson.

Women's Community Club.... A large crowd of our neighbours and friends is present and the Community House is being dedicated to the harmony, contentment and happiness of this district. May it be a source of inspiration to us, leading to a broader charity, a truer culture and a greater loyalty to our neighbours." It also listed the names of club members, names that remain in the community today either on rural road signs or the gates to descendants' farms.

In the summer of 2008, the Round Lake Community Recreation Society met and mustered the strength to tackle the Round Lake Hall. Mel Coulsen spearheaded community efforts to find grants and raise funds to completely renovate the hall from foundation to rafters. Indoor washrooms were necessary to update the building and a "flush fund" raised $16,000. Substantial grants from federal, provincial and local sources put $260,000 into the local economy. Five area residents were employed full-time for thirty-eight weeks, alongside a troop of subcontractors and talented community-minded volunteers.

In the summer of 2009, Round Lake Hall was officially re-opened in a grand ceremony attended by a crowd of three hundred people. There were speeches

Project Supervisor Bill Harness (right) works with fellow Quick residents Roxana Ross and Sheila Stewart on the most recent renovations to the hall. Photo by Dina Hanson.

St. John the Divine Anglican Church

St. John the Divine Anglican Church was built in 1914 as a testament to the faith of the people of Hubert. Constructing a building at that time in Hubert showed not only the faith of the parishioners but the faith that the newly established community up the Bulkley River from Telkwa would flourish. Hubert was built by optimistic settlers who hoped that the Grand Trunk Pacific would establish their divisional point there. When the railway declared in 1913 that Smithers was the chosen stopping place for freight and passengers, Hubert's future did not look bright. The farmers who had painstakingly cleared land, and the entrepreneurs who had built hotels and stores were disappointed, but they didn't abandon their little community. Many stayed on for years farming and living on the west side of the Bulkley

River. But over time the people moved away and the useable buildings were dismantled and brought elsewhere. St. John the Divine was a solid building and the residents in Quick resolved to move the church to Quick. In the fall of 1928, Jack Letchford and Angus Trail dismantled the building. Hilary Wearne wrote in *Bulkley Valley Stories* that "they took down each short piece of panelling and numbered it, ready to be put back together like a jigsaw puzzle." The church, now in carefully marked pieces, was loaded into a boxcar at the Hubert siding and taken to the Quick Station. "When we were taking off the inside walls," recalled Mr. Letchford while speaking to Hilary Wearne, "we both admired the good and neat carpentry work that went into the joining of the pieces, and the true straight cut of the rafter joints and framework." A Quick dairy farmer, R. McGregor, donated land for the St. John the

Divine Church on the corner of the Quick country road and the highway. With the help of the other neighbourhood volunteers, Letchford and Trail rebuilt the church. "It shows the high degree of craftsmanship and devoted work on the part of the two builders," wrote Wearne. Area farmers replaced the carved oak rails and engraved an eagle on the lectern. A pioneer cabinetmaker and farmer, Mr. Morin, built and donated the altar. William Greene of Meadowbrook Farm made and gifted the large wooden cross. The bell in the belfry is an old engine bell from an old steam engine.

The small heritage church still stands hidden behind tall aspens on the corner of Highway 16 and Quick Road West. The church and grounds are still cared for by the community. Once a month there is a service, and weddings are held occasionally. Every Christmas there is a wonderful candle-lit service.

by local government representatives, pioneers of the Quick community and members of the Wet'suwet'en Nation.

This grand re-opening was a bustle of activity with musicians rallying the crowd and children racing around the grounds in impressive packs. The hall is now complete with modern kitchen and bathrooms, and the Quick community has been strengthened by realizing the common goal of preserving its historic hall.

It should come as no surprise that our wedding anniversary party is in the planning, and what better spot than the newly renovated Round Lake Hall. This time there will be no need for a human wind-shield around the barbecues—there's a great kitchen inside—and no more water jugs on stumps by the outhouses.

Thanks to community-minded citizens, the Round Lake Hall has survived the years and transitioned gracefully into the twenty-first century.

MAKING TRACKS—BUILDING THE GRAND TRUNK PACIFIC RAILWAY

April 7, 1914, was a warm sunny day in northern British Columbia. People travelled along the muddy spring trails, some on foot, some in wagons and some on horseback. They were going to Fort Fraser for the last spike ceremony, marking the completion of Canada's second transcontinental railway, the Grand Trunk Pacific Railway (GTP). Ten years earlier in March 1904, the first president of the GTP, Charles Hays, stood before a meeting of shareholders and preached the advantages of a northern rail route as only an optimistic visionary could. Hays said the railway would open up the north, providing access to mineral wealth, large stands of timber and the agricultural potential of the land. He believed investing in the prospective townsites would be wise, because the railway would encourage settlement and travel among the new towns. The envisioned crowds of eager settlers needed a way to travel and an efficient way to transport their goods, and the GTP was the answer. Hays was especially fond of the planned city of Prince Rupert, which he said would quickly grow from barren land into a port metropolis to rival Vancouver.

The board of directors believed in Charles Hays and construction began on the prairie section of the railway in 1905. By 1908 construction had pushed

April 7, 1914. Railway officials, workers and local folk gathered to watch the track-laying teams from the west and the east as they raced towards the point of completion, where the last spike would be driven. Photos courtesy of Bulkley Valley Museum, P0339 (top), P0345 (bottom).

westward as far as Edmonton. The crews made good progress and crossed from Alberta into BC in November 1911. Over the next three years they built onward, to and through the newly established city of Prince George. Construction began eastward from the terminus of Prince Rupert in 1908. This piece of the railway, from Prince Rupert to Hazelton, proved to be the most difficult section of track ever laid in North America. Railway construction along the Skeena River was very challenging and slow. The rail bed was situated between the rising and falling Skeena River on one side and massive rock mountains on the other. Over twelve million pounds of explosives were needed to build the eighty-mile section of track between Rupert and Kitselas Canyon. A substantial amount of rock was blasted away to create the rail grade and build tunnels, three of which are four hundred, seven hundred and eleven hundred feet long. There were many bridges built over temperamental streams and creeks. Bridges that took many men years to build now take just a few seconds to cross. Snow slides, rockslides, floods and tunnel collapses resulted in fatalities and narrow escapes. The rough terrain and challenging work continually set back construction schedules. Work camps were established every two miles along the route. Food and shelter and even medical services varied according to which sub-contractor was in charge of the camp, and how financially supported he was by Foley, Welch and Stewart, the main contractors for the GTP. Foley, Welch and Stewart struggled to retain workers. For every man arriving in a camp, at least one was leaving. Wages of $2.50 to $3.75 per day for eight to ten hours' work were simply not competitive enough to retain most workers. The workers of the day referred to the F.W. and S. Company as "Fool'em, Work'em and Starve'em."

Newspaper accounts during this time point to inadequate camp conditions, shortages of food, supplies and equipment. One camp was described as having bunkhouses "… so filthy even a self-respecting pig would refuse to die in them." The camps on the western end faced the challenge of importing their supplies by sternwheeler from Prince Rupert; they were all at the mercy of the changing water levels of the Skeena River. Goods would be ordered for camp but a wait of months for them to arrive was not unusual. Some goods were transported over

Leslie Martin and Bernice Medbury Martin

When I worked at the Bulkley Valley Museum in Smithers, BC, I read, catalogued and filed away in the archives letters written by Bernice Medbury Martin. Bernice was the wife of a Grand Trunk Pacific Railway contractor, Leslie Martin. Bernice came north in 1912 to British Columbia and lived with her husband in various camps along the construction route. While she made butter, mended clothes, prepared meals from meagre supplies and watched the extremes of railway construction she wrote letters home to her family in Wisconsin. Her letters captured a unique woman's perspective on the rock-blasting and railroad-building that took place from 1912 to 1914.

Hardscrabble BC, Camp 22, Mile 112, Thursday March 14, 1912.

My dear family,

When I tell you about the roadbed here you will understand something of what this travelling is like. Up here, where the train stopped to let me off the night I came, the snow was shovelled off, the ties dumped out and the rails spiked down. The road bed is tilted so much they were such the boxcars would tip.

Opposite: Bernice Medbury Martin holding kittens at her home in Decker Lake. Photo courtesy of Bulkley Valley Museum, P2843. Above: Mrs. Ross, Bernice and Mrs. Sprauge. Photo courtesy of Bulkley Valley Museum, P0537.

They tucked some cord wood, kitchen stove sized, under the ties on the down end. Some places a lady's step apart, some a man's step and some (woe is me) [more] than my jumping distance in my blue skirt.

Goodnight, best love and don't be sorry for me,

Bernice

Bernice's daughter Lesley donated the collection of letters to the Bulkley Valley Museum. In 2010 Caitlin Press published *The Railroader's Wife: Letters from the Grand Trunk Pacific Railway* and Bernice's wonderful letters about the construction of the railway through northern BC became available for everyone to read and enjoy.

the rough track to the end of the rails, then hauled by man or horse upriver to the various camps.

The Grand Trunk Pacific and Foley, Welch and Stewart had five sternwheelers operating on the Skeena River between Prince Rupert and Hazelton. They were named the *Operator*, the *Conveyor*, the *Port Simpson*, the *Distributor* and the *Skeena*. These paddleboats were dedicated to hauling freight to the end of steel and the construction camps beyond. Tens of thousands of tons of railway construction materials and camp supplies were brought upriver this way, fighting through rapids and canyons with names like Hornet's Nest, Devil's Elbow and Whirly Gig. First Nations men, who knew the Skeena best, worked on some of the sternwheelers securing tow ropes to ringbolts and restocking the boats with wood for the engine. Due to a continual shortage of workers, labour disputes, extreme conditions and very challenging terrain, the rails didn't reach Hazelton until 1912, four years after construction began in Prince Rupert. At the same time the tracks were being laid over the newly constructed Skeena Crossing bridge in April 1912, Charles Hays was one of the unfortunate passengers on the *Titanic* and drowned at sea. The death of the GTP president was a blow to the company; he was the stubborn visionary for the railway's "mountain section." But the work continued. With the Skeena River behind them, the workers progressed eastward with contracts being let in sections all along the proposed line. The rail grade was built, rocks moved, creeks and rivers crossed, and cuts filled. Goods travelled along First Nations trails and rough wagon roads to the various camps or along the rough track to the end of steel. Roadhouses and ranches were scattered throughout the area. Camp conditions improved with easier access to the pioneer communities of Hazelton and Aldermere, the newly established village of Telkwa, and the soon-to-be town of Smithers. Progress was steady eastward past Barrett Ranch and along the new settlements of Decker Lake and Burns Lake. The end of steel had neared Fort Fraser by April 1914.

On April 6, R.A. Harlow, an engineer who worked on various contracts through the Bulkley Valley section, had knelt in the mud and marked the designated point of completion. An equal distance was measured on either side, and the track-laying teams from the east and the west were shown their starting marks for the race to the point of the last spike. The next day, April 7, people travelled from all around to see the last spike ceremony of the Grand Trunk Pacific Railway. A train came from the west with prominent passengers and railway officials, and another arrived from the east with chairmen, head engineers, board commissioners and managers of the GTP. Officials in crisp black suits stood in the mud amidst the melting snow. Behind them stood rows of working men in overalls, watching the crews as they feverishly laid the tracks for the last section of the railway. The two teams raced towards each other; it was the team from the east that finally won. Short rails were cut and secured in place to bridge the gap, and GTP President Edson Chamberlain drove the last spike in Canada's second transcontinental railway. At a cost of $112,000 per mile, the Grand Trunk Pacific Railway was complete. Mr. Chamberlain then presented a gold watch to each of the two men in charge of track laying, and R.A. Harlow painted "Point of Completion, April 7th, 1914" on the last rail. The rail was later taken up, sliced into paperweights, engraved, and given to GTP officials. The main line was cleared of work trains, and the president's train, with seven coaches and a dining car and decorated with ribbons, headed for Prince Rupert. This was the first train to cross the newly completed line. The *Interior News* reported that it swept along the line "like a giant meteor with rainbow trimmings." Despite shortages of workers, obstacles of terrain and tragedies, the Grand Trunk Pacific railway had been completed, and the vision of deceased GTP president Charles Hays was realized.

MAIN STREET, SMITHERS, BC

On March 28, 1913, the *Omenica Herald* out of Hazelton announced "The board of Railway Commissioners at Ottawa has approved of the station site at 'Smithers,' the second divisional point East of Prince Rupert, Mile 226.5.... The townsite will be for sale in August 1913...." Like so many other whistle stops along the railway, Smithers was named for a director of the Grand Trunk Pacific Railway (GTP). Sir Alfred Waldron Smithers, the chairman of the board of the railway at the time, had the honour of having the flat, swampy land at the base of Hudson Bay Mountain named after him.

In 1913 there were Wet'suwet'en living throughout the wider area, pioneer farmers were homesteading in the valley, and miners had established claims nearby. Aldermere, Telkwa and Hubert were existing settlements, and Prince Rupert was a well-established coastal city. But Smithers in 1913 was just a swamp. When the GTP decided upon Smithers as the switching point for steam engines and transferring of freight and passengers, they knew the divisional point would mean a settlement of significance. Settlers, entrepreneurs and prospective landowners had been awaiting the announcement, knowing that where freight was exchanged and passengers had to spend a night, there would be stores, hotels, homes and ultimately a guaranteed investment.

Bulkley Valley Museum curator Michelle Reguly explains that Smithers was laid out in typical railway fashion with the large train station forming the end of

Some of the earliest dwellings in Smithers. Jimmy's Lodging House, the McArthur Store, the Road House and the Union Bank are visible. McArthur's was the first store in Smithers. Photo courtesy of Bulkley Valley Museum, P0214.

a wide main street. During this time, town planners were laying out streets to accommodate the traffic of the day—the six- and eight-horse teams. The wide street was built to allow for the parking and turning around of horses and wagons.

Smithers' Main Street was the focus of significant investor attention. Prior to town lots going on sale, entrepreneurs had moved to the swamp and conducted business out of shacks and canvas tents.

"It was muddy and wet," says Reguly. "Ditches were dug to try to drain the water table." A massive ditch referred to as "The Grand Canal" ran the entire length of Main Street. "In places it was over four feet deep." Boardwalks kept people out of the mud, and planks allowed them to cross the "Canal."

Museum records tell of brides arriving from afar, alone or with children in tow, to be reunited with their husbands. They had left behind trolleys or cobblestone streets, only to step off the passenger train at Smithers and see the wide mud track that was Main Street, with just a scattering of tents and buildings. Despite

Smithers two months before lots were offered for sale. Photo courtesy of Bulkley Valley Museum, P2599.

Pioneering Smithers residents stop along the boardwalk outside Sargent's General Store. Visible in the distance is Mason Adams' Drug Store; this building remains today on the corner of Main Street and 2nd Avenue. Photo courtesy of Bulkley Valley Museum, P0375.

their shock, many women stayed, settled into their newly constructed homes and helped to literally build the town.

The buyers and builders were a hot topic, and local newspapers reported on the rapid progress of construction in the new town of Smithers. Just two months after lots went on sale there, Hazelton's *Omenica Miner* wrote "… over three hundred men are engaged in erecting permanent buildings… twenty-five blocks in the business centre have been cleared." There was a sawmill at this time, the Seymour Lake Lumber Company, that was reputed to be turning out ten thousand feet of lumber every day to keep up with the building boom. Smithers was transformed from swampy land with canvas tents and shacks to what the *Omenica Miner* described in October 1913 as "the best district in British Columbia." Very quickly the purchased lots on Main Street were made into cafés such as the Oyster Bay Café, accommodations like James Girling's large rooming house and the Carr Brothers' grand Bulkley Hotel, and Dr. C.G. MacLean's medical building.

Just one month later, the newspaper reported:

Early Smithers businesses being constructed: a mix of temporary canvas tents with a ready pile of build-ing materials. These wide ditches ran down Main Street and along the side streets. Photo courtesy of Bulkley Valley Museum, P0163.

Smithers now possesses graded streets, sidewalks, a post office, six rooming houses, five restaurants, four general stores, two churches, two newspapers, a bank, doctor, dentist, drugstore, hardware store, sawmill, planing mill, two lumber yards, plumber, sheet iron worker, sign works, three contracting firms, two laundries, two poolrooms, livery stable, meat market, electrical supply, shoe shop, two real estate firms, etc.

Today—and it is hard to believe the photographs of 1913 and 1914—Smithers' Main Street is paved, with four-way stops, wide sidewalks, benches, and mature trees and shrubs. The train station remains trackside but it is obscured behind the more modern courthouse building. Few of the original buildings remain on Main Street—most were lost to fires that destroyed entire sections of the street through the years. Others were lost to demolition and gave way to newer modern struc-tures built on their lots.

Central Park Building, Smithers. Photo courtesy of Bulkley Valley Museum, P2074.

Central Park Building, Smithers

In 1925 in Smithers, BC, a 7,700-square-foot provincial government building was completed. It was a huge structure for its day, with high ceilings on the two levels, and a third floor for residences and a big coal boiler in the basement. The provincial government building housed the courthouse, police station, jail and government agent. It was similar in size, shape and matched the exterior brown and white colouring of the Smithers train station, which was seven blocks away on Main Street.

These two buildings looked so similar they were referred to as the "bookends" of the Smithers Main Street.

On January 29, 1926, the provincial government building courthouse was officially opened and for five decades every birth, death, marriage, mining claim and land staking was heard within the walls. The men's and women's jail was located on the main floor of the building and up in the narrow hallways of the third floor lived the RCMP sargent and his family. The land commissioner, gold commissioner and provincial assessor were located in the building.

The government departments vacated the building in 1973 and it was donated to the Town of Smithers. They rented it out for a few years but soon the building was found to be in need of significant repairs and council considered demolition in 1974. In 1979 the Central Park Building Society took it over and significant repairs were carried out by volunteers. The former provincial building, now referred to as the Central Park Building, received heritage building status in 1980. Briefly in 1982 the fire department had to close it to the public and the historic building was almost demolished. But town council gave a group of volunteers a chance to upgrade the structure and they did. Significant expensive and extensive repairs were carried out in order to bring the former provincial government building up to date. The Central Park Building found tenants. A dance studio was opened in the former courthouse, the Smithers Art Gallery took over the government agent's room and the jail became the Bulkley Valley Museum with its archives stored in the walk-in government safe. The building remains a fixture on the corner of Highway 16, the major transportation corridor for the north, and Main Street, Smithers.

In celebration of the 100th anniversary of Smithers in 2013, a centennial committee has focussed some of their efforts upon a vacant Main Street corner lot. It is fitting that part of the centennial celebrations focus on Main Street—Main Street was and still is an important part of what makes Smithers unique. And, as curator Reguly says, "In just 100 years look how far we've come!"

THE FRED BUTTON NOTEBOOKS

T hanks to the astute observation of a library patron and quick action by the librarian, Prince Rupert acquired a collection of photographs from the city's early years.

In January 2009, the Prince Rupert City and Regional Archives received a number of phone calls about a new listing on eBay: local historians and Prince Rupert collectors were abuzz with news that a number of original Fred Button images had appeared for sale. Someone who had been watching eBay on the computer at the public library told librarian Kathleen Larkin, who then contacted the archivist for the Prince Rupert City and Regional Archives, setting in motion a process that concluded with the acquisition of this important collection.

Just who was Fred Button, and why were his old photographs creating such a stir in Prince Rupert?

According to records at the Prince Rupert City and Regional Archives, Fred Button was born in England in December 1877 to Sarah and William Button. In 1904, at age twenty-six, he married his wife, Louise. They immigrated to Canada in 1905, settling in Lethbridge, Alberta, in 1906.

At this time there was much speculation about northern BC and the talk of the Grand Trunk Pacific Railway constructing a route through the north. Fred may have heard about the prospects of the northern coast and the potential land and retail boom that construction would bring. The Buttons gathered the courage

Fred Button moved to Prince Rupert during its earliest years and recorded much of the city's early development in photographs. He left the area permanently in 1919. This photo, taken in 1918, courtesy of Prince Rupert City and Regional Archives, 2009.040.480.

to move to the newly established pioneer port city of Prince Rupert. Fred began photographing the very start of the city, and by 1909—the year Prince Rupert was founded—was issuing souvenir postcards showing Prince Rupert and area.

Like so many of the early settlers, Button had more than one occupation. He and Louise occasionally travelled and worked as Methodist missionaries on the Queen Charlotte Islands (now Haida Gwaii). In Prince Rupert, Fred worked as a real estate and insurance broker; in 1915, the F. Button Real Estate business was located on Second Avenue. He also became a well-travelled photographer, developing and selling postcards and prints.

Little is known about Button's life in Rupert. He shows up infrequently in the early newspapers and was not an active member in the town's early clubs or societies. But from his extensive black-and-white souvenir photographs and postcards we can tell Button travelled all along the railway construction line and over the pack-trails of northern BC, searching out the postcard-perfect photograph. Button followed and photographed the large coastal steamers and the smaller Skeena River sternwheelers. Through his photographs he documented the rise of the city of Prince Rupert, the boom of businesses and the sense of optimism that encompassed the settlers during the early years of construction of the railway.

Button used an early camera that allowed him to write directly on the image by using a small metal tool to scribe letters. On his hundreds of images Button etched his signature markings: the photo number, the photo description running along the bottom of the image and "F. Button, Prince Rupert," usually in the lower right-hand corner of the image. He was careful with his photographic collection, storing his negatives in between the pages of nine school notebooks.

Postcards would have been a popular item with the many new settlers to Prince Rupert and area. Not only did people make it a hobby to collect postcards, there were hundreds of newcomers who sent postcards back to their former homes. A picture postcard offered the new settlers an easy way to show their relatives and friends back home the massive wilderness of northern BC and the rapid scale of growth of the rising city of Prince Rupert.

Fred Button's photo documents the results of a tree falling on the *Operator*, a sternwheeler on the Skeena River. Photo courtesy of Bulkley Valley Museum, P2414.

In 1919 Fred left Prince Rupert for Texas. The *Evening Empire* of July 22, 1919, stated that "Mrs. Fred Button leaves tonight on the *Camosun* for Burkburnett, Texas, where Mr. Button is located."

The Prince Rupert City and Regional Archives records show that after five years in Burkburnett, Fred and Louise moved to Lubbock, Texas, where Fred tried his hand at another occupation, opening "Uncle Sam's Store," a grocery located on their Main Street. Louise died in 1953, and Fred died in 1962, at the age of eighty-four.

Button's nine notebooks stuffed with nitrate negatives, glass-plate negatives and loose film, spanning ten years of northern BC history from 1909 to 1919, were acquired by a collector with the name of Williams in Lubbock, Texas, where Button last lived. When Williams passed away, his daughter sold the notebooks to Rolf Hein of Pioneer, California, a dealer in "... books, ephemera, relics and historical collectibles." Having bachelor's degrees in both history and fine art, and over twenty years' experience as a collector, Mr. Hein immediately recognized the historical and artistic value of Button's images.

When archivist Jean Eiers-Page was contacted by the Prince Rupert librarian in January 2009, she immediately emailed the seller of the eBay items and "... advised him that the Prince Rupert City and Regional Archives, which is a non-profit society, would be very interested in acquiring the entire collection." Eiers-Page also asked the seller what the collection consisted of and the condition of the nitrate negatives. Hein replied with the news that he had approximately 550 of Button's negatives, and not only were they in great condition but he had been hoping an archives would contact him. Mr. Hein quickly provided an inventory of the negatives and emailed a photo of the notebooks.

In late January 2009, the board of directors of the Prince Rupert Archives met to discuss acquiring the collection and passed a motion to make the purchase. The sum of $1,125 in US funds was paid for the Button collection—an unusually large amount since most of the material obtained by the Archives is donated. "In rare cases, if a valuable collection does come up for sale, the Archives will try and scrape up funds and monetary donations for it," says Eiers-Page. "In this case the content of the negatives was a valuable asset to the history of Prince Rupert."

Going through the collection for the first time Eiers-Page was amazed at the great condition of the almost hundred-year-old negatives. As a professionally trained archivist, she knows that the best way to store negatives is away from air and out of the light, just as Button had done by pressing them flat between his notebook pages. Most of the negatives were numbered in signature Button style and were still in their original order. The staff at the Archives catalogued the collection, scanned all the negatives and placed them in acid-free envelopes.

The Prince Rupert City and Regional Archives put together a book for the 100th anniversary of Prince Rupert entitled *Prince Rupert: An Illustrated History*, making use of many of Button's fantastic photos.

The Button images are a great treasure that help us piece together our past. And, at just two little shoeboxes worth, the Button collection is now part of a much larger assortment of material that the Prince Rupert City and Regional Archives cares for that includes books, diaries, ledgers, art, films, tapes, slides, photos, negatives, microfilm, reference files, maps, plans, reference books and ephemera.

DORREEN, BC

Approximately thirty miles northeast of Terrace, across the Skeena River from Highway 16, is the historic community of Dorreen. There, running along the railway track from the old station to the railway bridge over Fiddler Creek, are the remains of a community that at first glance seems to have been simply left behind. Alders grow on the flat deck of an old round-fendered truck, horse-drawn farm implements peek out from the bracken ferns, a one-room schoolhouse sits vacant. But it wasn't always like this.

This area, where Fiddler Creek and Lorne Creek join the Skeena River, is the traditional territory of the Gitxsan. In the 1880s, this area hosted a frenzy of gold seekers. Chinese and European miners were recorded living on the west side of the Skeena at Lorne Creek, upriver from Dorreen, in 1884. They sluiced and panned the creek gravels—as many as 180 miners in 1885. Most of the prospectors' efforts were not rewarded and the gold boom at Lorne Creek went bust by 1888. The majority packed their bags and moved on to the next rumoured gold creek.

Those who stayed applied for land and homesteaded. A farm was established at the turn of the century and a hotel was built at Lorne Creek. In 1904 a hydraulic mine started, employing some of the settlers. The hardiest pioneers cleared land and overwintered on the west side of the Skeena in the area that soon became known as Dorreen and District.

Much of Dorreen was underwater in the flood of 1936. Here a young Denis Horwill stands in the boat with his dog Buster, while Denis's father, William (at right), and Pete McNichol keep dry on a float. The Dorreen General Store, owned and operated by the Horwills, is in the background. Photo by Jack McCubbin, courtesy of Denis Horwill.

The Grand Trunk Pacific Railway started construction along the Skeena from Prince Rupert in 1909, and by 1911 the right-of-way was being cleared towards Fiddler and Lorne Creeks. The railway changed the communities, bringing an influx of camp workers, then the settlers who were working for or relying on the railway. The railway assigned place names along the route, and the large area that Charles Carpenter—one of the early gold seekers—originally homesteaded became Dorreen.

Many assume that the town was named for a wife or daughter of a railway official, but in Dorreen's case it was named after Mr. Ernest James Dorreen, a resident engineer on the railway. Mr. Dorreen was originally from New Zealand. He staked claims in the area and worked on the Bulkley bridge railway crossing until 1914.

The early newspapers out of Terrace and Hazelton announced the news of the various small communities and the title "Dorreen and District" covered the

Old vehicles and other relics from bygone days peek through the ferns around the old townsite. This car, an old Volkswagen Karmann Ghia, is on Jane Stevenson's rural retreat property in Dorreen, BC. Photo by Matt J. Simmons.

comings and goings of the people at Pacific, Dorreen, Lorne Creek, Ritchie and Cedarvale, all particularly remote railway communities.

Dorreen became a permanent community as a result of the railway. It had a station, a siding, and a reliable route in and out for people and supplies to move to and from the larger communities of Terrace and Smithers. This brought a few new settlers to the area who purchased land from Charles Carpenter and established homes. The men often prospected and farmed in the summers; in winter many worked at cutting and hauling cedar poles to the Dorreen siding for shipping out on railcars.

Denis Horwill was born in 1924 to Florence and William Horwill, who operated the general store in Dorreen. The Dorreen Store was the community hub and the Horwills served as the post-mistress, sub-mining recorder and Justice of the Peace. Denis recalls the family also had a milk cow, shipping milk on the train to nearby Pacific, and produced food in their large gardens and greenhouse, shipping bedding plants to Terrace every spring. This was the era the mine operated in the mountains above Dorreen; a mine road was built and an aerial tram constructed to bring high-grade gold ore down the mountain to the railway.

There were prospectors in the hills, driven down to Dorreen only by the cold autumn weather. Newspapers referred to prospectors keeping secrets about their claims, but "there is no doubt they have something good, for their enthusiasm betrays them," observed the *Omineca Herald* in 1924.

Horwill explains that the 1930s were a tough time for many people: "With the crash in 1929 there just wasn't employment in many places." People came by railcar to Dorreen thinking they could find gold; some stayed and homesteaded permanently while others moved on after one season.

During the 1930s, Dorreen offered affordable shelter, a school and casual employment—farming and prospecting in the summer and pole-cutting in the winter. People dug wells, farmed, cooked on wood stoves and generally relied upon themselves and each other for their survival and entertainment. Dances were held in the schoolhouse; card games went on all night by the light of oil lamps. The isolation in Dorreen created a strong community where people were trusting and generous. Denis Horwill says of his family's general store, "I don't think the door was ever locked."

Dorreen was never a boom-and-bust town; it always just survived. Highway 16 was completed on the opposite side of the river from Dorreen in 1944, which meant people and traffic could move east and west without going through the settlement. It was the end for other railway communities, but not for Dorreen because a mine invested in the mountains above Dorreen in 1949. The school operated sporadically through the 1940s but closed permanently in 1953 when the mine shut down. William Horwill passed away in 1958 and his wife, Florence, continued to operate the store and post office until 1960. Economics changed and isolated little Dorreen, with just seasonal employment and subsistence farming,

Stopping at Lorne Creek

In 1909 a young man named F.C. Chettleburgh took the *Port Simpson* sternwheeler up the Skeena River from Prince Rupert to Hazelton. In those days the men on the sternwheelers were expected to get off the boat as required to help load and stack wood consumed by the steam power. Many passengers on these early Skeena sternwheelers remarked that they had heard of working for their passage aboard a vessel but never working and paying for passage. *Port Simpson* passenger Chettleburgh was recorded in the 1960s and he recalled, "We were loading wood, I was a young fellow at the time and I went out and helped." Chettleburgh found himself quickly soaked with sweat from the exertion and after the wood was aboard the sternwheeler he went and changed his shirt and overalls. In his clean clothes Chettleburgh made his way to the pilothouse to visit with the captain. "He [the captain] reached up to pull the bell rope, I said, 'Good God man you're not going to put on more wood?!'" The captain reassured the passenger, "'No, no,' he said, 'when I'm ahead like this I always drop off and see old George Carpenter at Lorne Creek, we always have a game of crib.'" True to his word, just one game later Chettleburgh recalled that the captain was back aboard and the *Port Simpson* churned its way up the Skeena River away from Lorne Creek and headed to Hazelton.

shrank slowly but steadily. There was a small resurgence of settlers in the late 1960s but that too did not last.

Dorreen was nominated for inclusion as a heritage site in the Regional District of Kitimat Stikine's Heritage Register. Planner Ken Newman hiked out to see just what is there—what the community looks like, what shape the buildings are in—and to get a sense of its layout and geography. "There is an intangible sense of place you gain from being there," he says. The old Horwills' store and the railway station are under consideration for heritage status in the regional district's register.

At first glance, Dorreen does seem deserted. But a closer look reveals a fresh coat of paint on the old station, houses that have been jacked up and brought to level. An examination of the visitor log-book tucked under the eaves of the general store's front porch reveals comments written by travellers from throughout the Northwest, many referring to the peaceful air and solitude. "It's nice to see that some things never change," says one.

Besides the seasonal citizens, there are two full-time residents. They like the place the way it is: quiet and isolated. If you manage to venture across the Skeena or find your way overland to the old townsite, remember that there are people living there—mowing lawns, tending gardens, chopping wood and pruning the hundred-year-old apple trees. Some of their buildings may be steadily leaning closer to the earth, and their cars haven't moved from the bracken ferns in decades, but the residents are full of life and want to see their community remain what it is—a reminder of the past with a life in the present, isolated and secure on the west side of the Skeena.

LILLIAN ALLING

Lillian Alling walked out of New York City in 1926, headed home—to Russia. She planned to walk as far as she could—the Bering Sea—and cross the ocean to the northeastern reaches of her homeland.

This incredible journey, some six thousand miles on foot, has given rise to many published stories, booklets, websites, inspired works of historical fiction and creative non-fiction, at least one song and even an opera that premiered in Vancouver in October 2010.

Lillian Alling's walk has inspired many researchers to trace her trail from New York City in 1926 to last sighting of her four years later near Teller, Alaska. Many have searched historical records, read old newspapers, and contacted museums along her long walking route and found it challenging to verify facts about her.

It is unanimous, though, that Alling came to New York City in the mid-1920s from Russia. Author Cassandra Pybus concluded that Lillian was a displaced Jew from Belorussia, and her not-so-Russian-sounding name "Alling" may have been "some derivation of Olejnik."

A small, fair-haired woman in her twenties with intense eyes and a determined spirit, Lillian found 1920s New York difficult to manage with no family or friends and English as her second language. She was frustrated with her various jobs. A 1941 article states that "the swift tempo of life bewildered her… [she] yearned once more for the rugged steppes of her native land."

When Lillian realized she could not afford steamship passage back to Russia, she decided to do what most would never even consider: she would walk. She studied maps at the New York Library and sketched her own plan. She set her determined mind to the massive undertaking: she would walk from New York to Chicago to Minneapolis, over the border into Canada and across the Prairies. She would then walk over the Rockies into BC and up to Hazelton to follow the Yukon Telegraph line north to Dawson, and on to the Bering Sea. The water crossing to her homeland of Russia looked deceptively easy on maps, especially when compared to the long overland journey.

It's hard to separate fact from fiction, but Calvin Rutstrum's articles state that Alling was seen in Chicago, then Minneapolis, then Winnipeg. The next confirmed reports of the lone woman walking are north of Hazelton on the telegraph line.

In the fall of 1927, the story goes, the telegraph linemen along the route knew that winter would soon arrive and that Lillian was not prepared. They tried to stop her, but when she continued north in spite of their warnings, they notified the police. Sergeant W.J. Service, in charge of the district, went out and brought Lillian to Hazelton. Journalist J. Wellsford Mills reports that at the Hazelton jail a matron searched Lillian and found she had no extra clothing, no matches, and no snowshoes—just three loaves of bread, some tea, twenty dollars and a short iron bar (which she said was to protect her not from bears but from men).

According to Mills, Sergeant Service, knowing Lillian would freeze or starve to death if she continued her journey, decided to lock her up. He charged her with vagrancy and recommended a fine he knew she could not pay. On September 21, she was sentenced to a fine of twenty-five dollars or two months in jail at Oakalla.

The Hazelton police and linemen thought Alling would go south, serve her time and stay in the city; surely she would come to her senses and never return. But in June 1928, Sergeant A. Fairbairn at Smithers was warned by Vancouver police that Lilllian had started travelling north. On July 19, she arrived in Smithers. Fairbairn realized this meant she had walked about thirty miles a day and he knew that with that pace she would likely reach the Yukon before winter arrived. The

Ogilvie Creek

Regional District of Kitimat Stikine planner Ken Newman elaborated on the story of Lillian Alling and the men Jim Christy and Charlie Janze at Cabin 8. Newman situates telegraph cabin No. 8 at about the mid-point of the trail between Hazelton and Telegraph Creek on Muckaboo Creek in the headwaters of the Nass River. Farther along the trail north of Cabin 8 is the treacherous Nass Summit and the Ningunsaw River. "Jim Christie and Charlie Janze communicated with the men north of them in the Echo Lake Cabin on the other side of the Nass Summit," explains Newman. They planned that Jim Christy from Cabin 8 would accompany Lillian over the Nass Summit and the men agreed that Scotty Ogilvie of the Echo Lake Cabin would walk the trail south to meet with Lillian. Echo Lake Cabin was a main battery station cabin. "It was from Echo Lake Cabin that Scotty Ogilvie left, travelling south to meet Lillian along the trail,"

Charlie Janze and pack dog. Photo courtesy of Bulkley Valley Museum, P0579.

says Newman. But tragedy struck. Before Ogilvie met up with Lillian, he attempted to cross Ningunsaw River when it was swollen from heavy rains. It was there, at the Ningunsaw River, that Scotty Ogilvie drowned.

Today Ogilvie Creek is a small creek named in honour of Scotty Ogilvie that flows into the Ningunsaw River just south of Echo Lake. Remains of the original Echo Lake telegraph cabin can still be found on the shores of Echo Lake not far off today's Highway 37.

police had no reason to stop her now, but asked her to check in with the linemen along the Telegraph Trail.

She did just that, and messages of her quick pace and short stays came from Cabins 1 through 7. Francis Dickie's article "New York–Siberia, the Astonishing Hike of Lillian Alling," states that when she reached Cabin 8 she was hungry, exhausted, eaten by blackflies, and the soles of her boots were worn right through. Jim Christie and Charlie Janze were stationed there and occupied one cabin each. Christie turned his cabin over to Lillian for three days and the men went to work, feeding her large meals and repairing her clothing.

Lillian had the linemen's support and they reported her progress to Echo Lake, the Iskut River and to the open country north of Telegraph Creek. When the linemen lost her trail as she walked to Atlin, the *Whitehorse Star* newspaper picked it up, reporting that Lillian arrived in Atlin in late August and bought a new pair of shoes. She continued walking, received a ride across the river at Tagish, then arrived in Carcross where she had a meal at the Caribou Hotel. She rested in Whitehorse briefly before heading out on the Dawson Trail on September 7, 1928.

The *Star* continued to report on Alling's progress: she was sighted east of Tahkinna, then at the Yukon River where H.O. Lokken helped her across. Another man, A. Shafer, helped her at Pelly River Crossing. An October storm hit at Stewart, and she was cared for by a survey party in their camp for three days. She caught a ride downriver on a small boat, reaching Dawson thirty-nine days after leaving Whitehorse—with a different style of men's shoe on each foot. A few published sources state that she had the hide of one of the lineman's pack dogs stuffed with grass on top of her pack (a fact that other articles disagree with, since she never stayed anywhere long enough to tan a hide).

Alling worked that winter in Dawson and repaired a small boat. As soon as the river broke up in the spring, Lillian was on her boat, making the sixteen-hundred-mile journey downriver to the Bering Sea.

Her trail breaks up at this point. Francis Dickie writes that "she reached the mouth of the Yukon safely... left her boat on the beach and trudged into the Arctic vastness." Several historians write that she was seen passing Tanana and arrived at Nome. Francis Dickie reports that, months later, an Eskimo reported seeing a woman pulling a two-wheeled cart beyond Teller, a coastal outport near a point where Alaska and Siberia are closest.

Arthur F. Elmore recounts that a Russian friend told him a story in 1965 when he was visiting Yakutsk, in eastern Siberia. His friend told him that when he was a young boy in the fall of 1930 in the Soviet Far East (Provideniya, 170 miles from the Bering Strait), he recalled seeing a young woman in American dress accompanied by Diomede Island Eskimos. Officials at the waterfront led her away, but he remembers hearing that the young woman had come from America, where she had been unable to make friends or get a good job. The Russian man had been deeply affected by the story and for many years felt that if he went to America he would also be poorly treated.

Lillian's story is fascinating—her against-all-odds walk across North America over mountain passes and through all kinds of inclement weather. The uncertainty of her journey's end does not lessen her story's appeal. Did she reach her homeland to see her supposed long-lost love, and reunite with her family? Did she perish at sea or turn back and live out her days in Alaska?

Some eighty-four years later, Lillian Alling's story has reached almost mythic proportions. It is the stuff of inspiration, as many writers, artists and even opera composers can attest.

SLIM WILLIAMS

Clyde "Slim" Williams travelled to Alaska in 1900 at the age of eighteen to prospect, and survived there by mining, trapping, delivering mail and raising sled dogs. In 1932, he boasted that his strong wolf-dog teams could mush all the way from his home in Copper Center, Alaska, to Chicago, and do it in time for the World's Fair of 1933.

Proponents of an Alaska highway route learned of Slim's boast and realized that such a feat would draw much-needed attention to their cause. Author Bill Miller, in his book *Wires in the Wilderness: The Story of the Yukon Telegraph,* writes that, "… one thing led to another, and he found that his original goal of visiting the Chicago World's Fair had been expanded to include blazing and publicizing the route for an international highway."

Slim was told that if he and his dogs could get to the Chicago World's Fair by its opening in September 1933, he could be the star of the show in his very own "Alaska Cabin" exhibit. He decided he was up for the Chicago challenge, but he also set his sights on Washington, DC, and meeting President Franklin D. Roosevelt.

Williams was fifty-one years old when he hitched up his eight-dog sled team and began his trip. "In November of 1932 Slim set out from Copper Center in minus 40° weather," writes Miller. His progress was followed with interest by small-town newspapers in BC, the Yukon and throughout the US. The US papers repeatedly overlooked the Yukon and British Columbia in their coverage. If they

Slim stopped briefly in Telkwa. Here his team rests on the retail street near the Bulkley River. One of the reasons for his journey was to raise support for the construction of a highway to Alaska. Photo courtesy of Telkwa Museum, P0465.

did mention BC or the Yukon, our mountains became the Canadian "Plains" and our well-established settlements became "unmapped" and "uncharted" territory, and a "frozen" one too. One American paper featured a photograph with the caption, "Williams by Yukon River on his way into Washington." The American press may have ignored the giant, populated Canadian land mass, but Canadians did not ignore Williams.

Miller explains that Williams went the "long way around, via Chicken, Forty Mile and Dawson City, then headed south to Whitehorse and eventually reached Atlin." He encountered deep snow and for hundreds of miles had to break trail, on snowshoes, for the dogs. On January 25, 1933, New Hazelton's *Omenica Herald* wrote, "Slim Williams is somewhere between White Horse YT and Atlin. He is on a trip by dog team from Alaska to Chicago. He will pass

Slim Williams leaving Telkwa in the spring of 1933, on his way to Chicago with his dogsled newly outfitted with wheels. Photo courtesy of Telkwa Museum, P0440.

through here en route. The distance from White Horse to Atlin is 500 miles (not short miles either) and it will be at least a month yet before he will hit the local part of the Yukon Telegraph line. Williams is going to the Chicago World's Fair and wants to get there for the opening."

On March 29, the paper wrote an extended piece, stating, "Slim Williams arrived at Hazelton on Tuesday afternoon safe and sound. After a rest of a couple of days he will resume his journey to Seattle and thence to Chicago to attend the opening of the world's fair. Williams is in good health and now that he is feeling over the worst of the trip he is feeling quite enthusiastic. He has averaged 13 miles a day since he left home and he figures that is pretty good going under the circumstances. He arrived at Second Cabin on the Yukon Telegraph trail last Sunday afternoon and soon after that took to the ice on the river. Slim says he has had a

Slim Williams travelling through the Bulkley Valley. Photo courtesy of Telkwa Museum, P0473.

wonderful trip thus far. It is the greatest game country he ever saw. It was quite common for him to see twenty moose in a day and nearly every day…. Williams arrived here to find the roads practically bare of snow and as a sleighing proposition from here to the south does not appeal to him, he has decided to rig his sleigh up with some wheels and proceed over the highway as soon as possible. He figures he will cover more miles per day now that he does not have to break trail."

Lillian Weedmark, former curator of the Bulkley Valley Museum in Smithers, researched Slim's brief time in Smithers and wrote, "He rigged the sleigh up with wheels from a narrowed Ford chassis. Local schoolchildren had been so excited by his visit that he waited on Monday until they were out of school so they could watch him leave." The *Interior News* recorded that there were over a thousand people on the streets to watch Slim and his wheeled dogsled leave Smithers; every corner was crowded. Weedmark wrote, "He drove up Broadway and went onto Main. The lead dog made the turn, but the rest of the team kept on going in the original direction and the new brake couldn't hold them. They ran over a ditch and came to rest behind a telephone pole." Repairs had to be made and he departed Smithers the next day. He was now clear of winter weather and, aside from mudholes, he made good time. As the weather warmed, Slim travelled mainly at night to spare the dogs the heat.

In the autumn of 1933, after mushing hundreds of highway miles, Slim arrived in Chicago in time for the World's Fair. On September 27, the *Omenica Herald* wrote that Williams was in Chicago: "… He was travel-worn and he and his dogs were tired and not favourably impressed by the hot weather." Slim and his dog team were hosts of the very popular "Alaska Cabin" exhibit at the fair before mushing on to Washington, DC, where Slim camped in city parks and spoke to President Roosevelt about the importance of an international highway.

In May 1939, Williams repeated his journey out of Alaska to the United States, but this time he brought only one dog and a fellow human traveller, John Logan from Portland, Oregon. And this time he left his sled at home and the two men opted for motorcycles. Extraordinarily, they filmed parts of their journey using colour silent film. The films are available online through Alaska's Digital Archives and show the two men constructing rafts to cross rivers, cooking over an open fire and even zipping around Hazelton. Weedmark wrote that Slim arrived in Hazelton in November and gave a speech to the Hazelton Chamber of Commerce saying that if the road wasn't built soon, his next trip would be by tractor. At Hazelton, the trail became a road in better condition and the two motorcycles were lashed together with a basket between for the dog. Making good progress, they arrived in Seattle in December.

Slim never did do the trip by tractor. Construction on the Alaska Highway began in 1942, spurred on by World War II. The route was not the one that Slim blazed though; this Alaska-Canada highway was built northwards out of Dawson Creek.

Later in life, Slim travelled the US as a lecturer, advertised as "The Alaskan Adventurer and Musher Who Became World Famous for Driving His Wolf-Dog Team 5,600 Miles Blazing the Proposed US Alaska Highway." He was billed as "Rugged, Picturesque, Humorous, Philosophical." After his lecture circuit, he moved back to Alaska and lived to be ninety-three.

SMITHERS DOMINION EXPERIMENTAL FARM

Imagine a farm in northern BC where you could wander through a field of winter wheat, examine forage crops, learn about poultry housing and read years of local weather records. At this farm you would find a supervisor, a manager agronomist, a clerk and a plethora of knowledgeable staff, all there especially for your education. They would happily tour you through their agricultural trials and share with you their lessons on what grows best in our local climate and how best to manage a farm.

It sounds so idealistic—I can almost see the bluebirds sitting on the fence posts and hear the gentle cows rustling in the fields—yet it was true. The Dominion Experimental Farm officially opened in 1937 on 320 acres just east of Smithers. Its purpose was to educate farmers and prospective farmers on how best to farm in our often-inhospitable northern climate.

As early as 1913, the *Interior News* reported on the need for an experimental farm to help the local farmers. The early settlers painstakingly cleared land by felling trees, blasting stumps, pulling roots and moving rocks. With little guidance and often no former experience they learned through trial and error. The 1913 article refers to the "many failures" of early agriculture and states, "what is needed is a northern experimental farm."

Local farmers experimented on their own with various crops and livestock, and formed groups and societies to share information. It wasn't until July 1937 that the Dominion Department of Agriculture bought the 320-acre Sproule farm for $5,500 and established the Smithers Dominion Experimental Farm.

The Experimental Farm was by all farming standards a major operation. It had livestock: cattle, hogs and sheep, work horses and poultry. Forage crops and cereals, including wheat, oats and barley, were grown. The farm had large gardens with vegetable crops, small fruits, tree fruits and ornamentals. Detailed records were kept on everything from egg production to fruit-tree diseases. The full-time staff of seven men in the winter and up to seventeen in the summer was completely dedicated to farm duties. There were even half a dozen workers busy all summer picking rocks from the fields.

Many local men were employed as carpenters to build the farm structures, outbuildings and residences. Many of these workers were from Holland and learned English while they worked—measuring and sawing boards, and mixing and pouring cement. The farm buildings were built according to federal government standards with deep cement footings, solid wood beams and a uniform colour scheme.

A report from 1950 states the Smithers Dominion Experimental Farm held "field days" in "order to help the farming public become better acquainted with the work underway... in an organized effort to make the results of the work known to all."

At one such field day in 1951, Johnny Zacharias led a group of thirty interested farmers through the fields at the farm. The *Interior News* reported that the farmers made lots of notes and later discussed "... whether it was better to sell forage crops or use them to fatten beef; whether there will be a reasonable market for milk in Kitimat; and whether or not fertilizer is as good as the experts say."

A Walter Burns was part of the field days, and led discussions about marketing and the challenges faced by our farmers. Mr. Burns had been appointed the

1913: A farmer uses horse power to help plow an already established field at Hubert east of Telkwa. Photo courtesy of Bulkley Valley Museum, P0021.

DOMINION EXPERIMENTAL FARM at
SMITHERS, B.C. PHOTO A.W.LENSER

The Dominion Experimental Farm was built near Smithers in the late 1930s. Photo courtesy of Bulkley Valley Museum, P0819.

superintendent of the experimental farm in 1938. He was dedicated to agriculture and worked on the Smithers substation farm for many years. In 1950 he wrote a detailed progress report for submission to Ottawa with information on raising farm crops and animals in our northern region. Barring the details on how to apply DDT to fruit trees and berry plants, many of the conclusions remain applicable today.

"The long winter feeding period," wrote Mr. Burns, "is a severe handicap to animal production." Despite noting that the "summers are short and the frosts frequent," he pointed out "the home garden is a very vital food source for the area." He goes on to list the best varieties of vegetables to grow in our region.

The experimental farm started scaling down employees and production in the mid-1950s. In 1957, a change in the federal government led to a tightened national budget and the eventual closure of the farm.

Construction of new buildings continued into the 1950s. The seed shed being built here still stands at the farm today. Photo courtesy of the Hofsink family.

What was once the experimental farm is now divided into smaller acreages, with Highway 16 running through the corner of them. You can catch a glimpse of some of the original cement fence posts and the old root cellar as you approach the curve near Babine Lake Road.

Between 1957 and today, the site has had many uses. In the late 1970s and early 1980s, it served as the Northern Training Centre, a vocational training residence for young people with disabilities. Young adults living at the facility managed a garden, raised pigs, and utilized a commercial kitchen. Eileen Klassen worked there from 1980–83 and recalls that the site was always busy, with up to twenty-six young adults living there and a steady wait-list.

From 1984–96, the site was home to the Residential Attendance Program, a facility staffed twenty-four hours a day for young offenders. The program offered counselling and focussed on improving these young adults' life skills.

Still later, the non-profit Smithers Community Services owned part of the property. During this time, the small farmhouses were rented out and a community garden and greenhouse were maintained on site.

The main part of the old farm, with its large barn, tall seed house, many outbuildings and small houses, is now owned by the Penninga family who have, through much effort, cleaned up the site.

The owners toured me through the old farm with its charming 1950s-style bungalows, the small creamery with its sunken floor for cold storage, and sheds with counterweighted sliding doors still riding smoothly more than fifty years after they were installed. The stunning hip-roofed barn, with its huge timbers and sunlight streaming through the holes in the original roofing, has just enough hay and manure smells remaining to hint at the pigs that used to live there.

The day I was there, swallows swooped around the rafters and laying hens happily ranged around the grounds. But there is no active farming today—it is a family home now, not buzzing with staff dedicated to farm activities. The Penningas and I stood in the shade of the old barn and discussed Mr. Burns and the old Dominion Experimental Farm. We acknowledged the work of Mr. Burns, who passed away aged ninety-three in April 2009. He dedicated his career to agriculture and was

Telkwa, an Agricultural Centre

Doug Boersema is a volunteer at the Telkwa Museum located on Highway 16 in Telkwa, BC. The Telkwa Museum is a former schoolhouse building packed with interesting artifacts from Telkwa and the surrounding rural area. Boersema knows the artifacts on display and in the storage area very well. He has stories about the photographs on display and family histories of some of the pioneer families that donated the artifacts.

Standing in front of one of the large glass cases that exhibits Telkwa Creamery butter wrappers, large churns and small rectangular wooden butter presses, Boersema says that Telkwa was once an agricultural centre for the Bulkley Valley. Farmers grew crops and exported their butter, eggs, seed potatoes and timothy seed on the Grand Trunk Pacific Railway. For many years, Telkwa was an important farming distribution centre and remained one even after Smithers was founded. "This valley was known for its high quality timothy," says Boersema. Area farmers grew timothy and sold huge amounts of the seed across Canada. Timothy was and still is an important element of a hay crop. There was such a demand for the Bulkley Valley timothy that settlers in Telkwa opened a seed-cleaning plant where farmers took wagonloads of their crop to have the seed separated from the husk. The farmers surrounding Telkwa, in the Quick and Round Lake area, secured large contracts to grow timothy and sell the high-quality timothy seed to larger distributors who re-bagged and sold the seed. "It was a big deal," says Boersema. He mentions the Letchford family as an example, which had a contract for delivering fifteen tons of timothy seed to the Eaton's company in Toronto. Boersema has studied the early issues of the *Interior News* and

Early stores along the riverfront in Telkwa, BC. The sign on the bluff advertises the New Telkwa Hotel. Photo courtesy of Telkwa Museum, P0694.

notes that the seed business must have been good, because in 1939 a major addition was built onto the seed-cleaning plant in Telkwa.

This was also the year that the Telkwa Creamery opened by the Bulkley River in Telkwa. Alfred Millar of Interior Creameries in Prince George opened a branch in Telkwa that was managed by Thor Paulsen. Those who once worked at the creamery say the butter they made in Telkwa was sold locally out of the cooling room as well as

exported on the train to general stores in the surrounding area and even farther away to larger centres. Boersema explains that area farmers brought their cream to Telkwa although some put their tall milk cans with their farm's name painted on them on the train to Telkwa. Cream was shipped daily on the CN Railway. The creamery would measure the butter fat content of the cream and pay the farmers according to the fat content as well as the taste and smell

WHEAT FIELD & RANCH NEAR SMITHERS

A successful crop at Diamond D Ranch. Photo courtesy of Bulkley Valley Museum, P2618.

of the cream. During the summer months, a surplus of 400,000 pounds of Bulkley Valley brand butter accumulated in the creamery's cold storage. This was sold out of the storefront, and to retail outlets, delivered to stores weekly.

At the Telkwa Museum, Boersema explains that the seed-cleaning plant slowed down during World War II and never regained a steady business. The Telkwa seed-cleaning plant building lived on, occupied by various businesses until it was demolished in 2010. The Telkwa Creamery and Bulkley Valley brand butter also suffered after World War II due to higher shipping costs, lack of government subsidies for farmers and dairy quota challenges. The Telkwa Creamery closed in 1969. It was the last independent creamery in British Columbia. The creamery building still stands beside the community outdoor ice rink right alongside the beautiful Bulkley River in Telkwa and has been for the last few years a fly fishing lodge.

awarded the Order of Canada for his work in Canada and abroad. We also talked about how many of the records from the old Dominion Experimental Farm have disappeared, possibly squirrelled away in a former employee's attic. But we hope that documents and images will resurface, providing the farmers and growers in the area with more advice and insights into the past.

In Burns' 1950s report, after many years of experimenting with crops and livestock and experiencing the challenges of northern farming first-hand, he wrote very frankly that the farmers in this area face some significant disadvantages: long winters, lack of water, poorer soils and distance to market. Despite the difficulties in growing crops and raising livestock here, Burns noted that there were many farms succeeding despite the odds against them. He attributed the fact that they did so well (and, I should add, continue to do so today) solely to the farmers' tenacity.

MENNONITE MIGRATION

In 1940, Saskatchewan was still struggling to recover from the Depression and was experiencing a severe drought. Soils were parched and seeds wouldn't germinate. With no crops to grow, farms and farm families were suffering. "Drought, dust, heat, grasshoppers, western equine encephalitis and army worms drove farmers to desperation," according to the Saskatchewan Archives Association.

At the time, the Saskatchewan government was providing relief payments to suffering families and wanted to move people off the drought-stricken prairie to raw land that could be farmed. In BC, meanwhile, the government wanted to see more people settled in the northern part of the province. Saskatchewan and BC worked together to move distressed families off the prairie and onto land that the BC government wanted to develop near Burns Lake.

"The government chose families who had experience, pioneering qualities, adequate livestock, and machinery," says Conrad Stoesz, archivist at the Mennonite Heritage Centre in Manitoba. The Mennonite families exemplified these qualities.

Stoesz, who has written about the migration of Mennonites from Saskatchewan to Ootsa Lake and Cheslatta, south of Burns Lake, says that in total 56 adults and 153 children left their prairie home to homestead in this area of BC. The Saskatchewan government paid for their transportation to their new home.

Helen Rose Pauls writes in *The Way We Were: First Mennonite Church, Burns Lake* that "the first Mennonite settlers in the Burns Lake area were Old Colony

Mennonites from the Hague–Osler and Toppingham areas of Saskatchewan." Their eight-hundred-mile move to Burns Lake was not easy. All their household effects, large farm implements (including tractors and entire blacksmith outfits), livestock, and they themselves had to be moved on the train. In the days leading up to the Mennonites' departure, the yards surrounding the prairie railway stations were crowded with wagons, tractors and horse-drawn farm implements.

Photographs show that on May 2 large groups of Mennonites gathered at the railway station in Toppingham, Saskatchewan; they arrived in Burns Lake about a week later. "The families came with various items such as ploughs, harrows, cream separators, horses, cattle, and chickens," says Stoesz.

At Burns Lake they unloaded the forty-four boxcars and drove trucks and wagons along the rough dirt roads out of Burns Lake. Trucks carried them for the first thirty miles, but the roads soon became impassable and the Mennonites turned to their horses and wagons. A dairy newspaper following their progress reported that fourteen miles of roads had to be re-built to permit the Mennonite wagons to pass; their first ten days in BC were spent working on the roads.

Another crowd of Mennonite families assembled at the Osler station in Saskatchewan the following month; a week later they were following the same dirt road—now improved by the families who preceded them—south from Burns Lake. The Mennonites were not going to existing farms with finished houses; theirs was the marginal raw land that earlier Southside settlers had passed over.

Although the Saskatchewan government provided the relocated Mennonites with support rations for up to three years, the families were remarkably quick to get established and comfortable in their new landscape. "Upon arrival, families toured in small groups with BC and Saskatchewan government officials to select specific tracts of land," says Stoesz. "Timber permits were secured allowing the families to obtain trees for building shelters and fences."

The settlers lived in temporary housing while they cut and peeled logs to build their homes and outbuildings. Photographs show that some erected prairie-style teepees for the remaining summer months. Helen Rose Pauls writes that, upon arrival in their new home, the Mennonites constructed two churches in

Mennonite settlers pass Tchesinkut Lake, south of Burns Lake. Mennonite Heritage Centre, Winnipeg.

Cheslatta and Grassy Plains. These were used as private schools for the children during the week. Working together, the families built log homes and log barns, and cleared, cultivated and cropped acres of land. Those who didn't have homes built lived with each other in temporary shelters until the following spring; one young family intended to spend their first winter in a granary they had brought with them from Toppingham.

An agent from the Department of Colonization and Agriculture of the Canadian National Railway in Winnipeg followed up with the Mennonites, visiting them in the summer of 1940 and assessing their "chances of success" in the Burns Lake district. He toured the area and recorded his observations of their situation. Frank appraisals were made of the settlers' characters; comments ranged widely from "settler is a good type" to "it is only through the influence and active assistance of his two relatives that he will eventually succeed." Some men found work cutting hay at established farms in the area, including the Bostrom Ranch, a well-established farm at Grassy Plains, where Mennonites J. Schapansky, Herman

Dick and C. Giesbrecht cut and put up the entire crop of timothy hay. Of the 160 loads of hay, Bostrom gave the workers half the crop.

The Saskatchewan government also sent an agent to check on the settlement of Mennonites south of Burns Lake. He noticed that the crops sown in June failed to reach maturity and would be good for animal feed only. Archivist Stoesz notes that, "in October, friends in Saskatchewan sent extra feed for the winter."

Stoesz refers to a "Directors Audit Report, Burns Lake District Office," which shows that the population of the Burns Lake region in 1940 was approximately 10,000 and that 30 per cent were part of the Mennonite community. The governments of BC and Saskatchewan took note of the successes of the Southside Mennonites; Stoesz adds that "in 1941 another 25 families were relocated to the Vanderhoof area of BC."

During a later inspection, the CNR Department of Colonization and Agriculture noted that, "by 1942 there were 400 acres under cultivation with crops giving good yields; they had big gardens and comfortable homes and no assistance was needed." The Mennonites had clearly settled in and were thriving on their new homesteads.

Pauls writes that after the first immigration of Mennonites in 1940, others followed: "Mexican Mennonites moved to the area to work in the mills, as did Sommerfelder Mennonites from the prairies and General Conference Mennonites from southern BC." There were also affiliations with the Eastern Pennsylvania Mennonites.

The provinces of BC and Saskatchewan saw the re-settlement of the prairie Mennonites as "highly satisfactory" and, had the Depression continued, more settlements would have been established to relocate more Mennonites. "This plan," says Stoesz, "provided drought-stricken families with a new start, cash-strapped provinces with a way of decreasing relief payments, and a way for BC to increase its northern population."

THE NO. 1 ARMOURED TRAIN— WORLD WAR II ALONG THE SKEENA

I was raised in northern BC in the 1980s. It was a peaceful time, and a positively serene place to grow up. Kitimat's tall and silent air-raid sirens were just a meeting place for neighbourhood kids.

I never feared an invasion; never considered a war. But Dad did point to the bunkers hidden behind cow-parsnip thickets near the Terrace airport. Mom did tell me about our Japanese neighbours driven from their coastal homes in a wave of suspicion. And schools did teach all the facts and dates of the world wars. But it wasn't until I saw photographs of an armoured train that operated along the Skeena River that I realized the extent of fear that must have blanketed northern BC during World War II.

As early as 1939, Prince Rupert was building up its coastal defences, with military forts built on Digby and Kaien Islands to defend the harbour against possible Japanese attack. Prince Rupert was at the end of the northern rail line and an important coastal staging area for troops and supplies going north to

Opposite: The armoured train included four armed gondola cars, which were equipped with a variety of munitions. Above: The train nearing completion, shown here in July of 1942 at Transcona, Manitoba. Photos courtesy Transcona Historical Museum and the Public Archives of Canada.

Alaska and the Aleutian Islands. American and Canadian troops were stationed there and they manned the forts, patrolled the shipyards and guarded railway bridges along the Skeena River. The entrances to Prince Rupert harbour were blocked by boats and submarine nets.

Jobs related to the war effort were easy to find, and Prince Rupert experienced a population boom. Military vessels were being built at the Prince Rupert dry dock and shipyard. A seaplane base, hangars and barracks were constructed for the air force.

In December 1941, the Japanese launched offensives against British, Dutch and American holdings in the central Pacific and Southeast Asia, including the attack on the American fleet at Pearl Harbor. Prince Rupert, situated on Canada's west coast and playing a role in the overall war effort, now felt especially vulnerable

A Child Remembers World War II

Roger Klein lived in Prince Rupert during World War II where his dad was working on the transport ships at the shipyards and also for the home guard as a shore defence gunner, manning a Bren gun. Klein recalled that at work his father wore a steel helmet and had a gas mask slung around his neck. There were reports at that time of submarines being sighted off Prince Rupert. "The big gun shore batteries used to practice with a huge salvo over Prince Rupert, at any time everything shook," Klein says. Klein has fond memories of watching the US air force planes fly over Prince Rupert on their way to Alaska. Hundreds of planes with loud aircraft engines—P38s and P40s—flew over in a low formation, a scene so impressive that as a young child, Klein decided he wanted to be a pilot.

The railway proved an important wartime route and figures in a child's remembrances of World War II: "I remember that every few days train after train, some loaded with soldiers in full kit, others speeding to the coast loaded up with tanks, aircraft with wings folded up wrapped up in tarps, artillery guns, army trucks and jeeps." Klein remembers, "my father used to take me to the rail station and one night he took me there to point out the 'skunk train' as he referred to it, that had a secret job to do." About the armoured train he says, "I can't remember if the whole train was there but the locomotive was what I was looking at, it was painted and looked so very different from all the other engines I had seen." Not far from the station, an army canteen operated and dances were held there to see off the young men before they shipped out.

Many of our early residents who lived not so long ago with the fear of war arriving on their doorstep, coming up the river and across the skies can recall this time with impressive clarity.

to attack. Barracks, mess halls, administration buildings and armouries were built and expanded. Airports were constructed at Terrace, Smithers and halfway between these two communities at Woodcock.

So heightened was the threat of Japanese invasion that in March 1942 the Department of National Defence and the CN Railway met to discuss the need for a specially constructed armoured train, built exclusively to patrol the Skeena River and protect the vital rail link.

In spring 1942, blueprints from Ottawa and materials from Halifax were shipped to the manufacturing shops at Transcona, Manitoba, and construction began on the No. 1 Armoured Train. Military men watched the labourers work three shifts a day, including Sundays and holidays, covering the rail cars in thick and heavy armour plate. In June 1942, while the armoured train was experiencing construction challenges from a lack of supplies and sudden design changes, the Japanese were ashore in the Aleutian Islands and an attack on Prince Rupert was thought to be imminent.

On July 21, the new armoured train, drawn by a steam locomotive, arrived in Terrace. There was no welcoming fanfare or press release; most residents did not even know of its existence. The massive train was made up of eight cars: two armed gondola cars followed by a coach for the soldiers, the locomotive in the centre, then a dining car and two more armed gondola cars bringing up the rear. With armour eight to sixteen millimetres thick, and carrying troops armed with mortars, guns and anti-tank rifles, the train patrolled the area between Terrace and Prince Rupert looking for any suspicious activity that could signify threat of Japanese invasion.

On the first trial run to Prince Rupert on July 29, 1942, a number of problems became apparent. The armour plating made the train very heavy, forcing it to operate much slower than expected. The track was in poor shape and the many curves slowed the train even more, down to less than ten miles per hour. The severe vibrations of the train caused bolts to loosen on gun mounts. The bulbs and the reflectors for the headlights had not yet been installed and there were problems with the searchlights. The crew had not been trained in advance, and the major general found them sullen and unenthusiastic. The troops disliked the

A soldier at his post above one of the infantry cars. Photo courtesy Transcona Historical Museum and the Public Archives of Canada.

close quarters and confined space; some went AWOL upon their arrival in Rupert. The radios went dead when the whistle sounded. The sighting scopes were hazardous to look through as the train was vibrating along the tracks. The weight of the train actually damaged the track and derailments occurred. But one major success was realized on that first run: despite much doubt, the gun mounts did clear the tunnels.

The trip one way from Terrace to Prince Rupert (about 95 miles) took the train twelve hours. The soldiers complained that the trip was too long, and their superiors agreed. In an effort to provide a rest on a long shift, and to train troops, the route was shortened some 25 miles by changing the endpoint from Prince Rupert to Tyee, at the mouth of the Skeena, where an attack was thought to be most likely. The soldiers watched for "the enemy" along the Skeena River—and saw not one sign.

Changes were recommended to improve the train: raising the gun mounts so they could fire towards the ground; providing safety chains to the men on top of the rail cars; fitting rubber eye cups on sighting scopes and providing better searchlights. In September 1942, the armoured train was sent to Vancouver for upgrades and returned in November.

By the end of 1942, when the new and improved armoured train operated between Tyee and Prince Rupert, the Japanese threat to the west coast was lessening. By January 1943, the No. 1 Armoured Train ran only once a week. During their days off, the crew carried out training exercises and target practice. In August 1943, US and Canadian troops reclaimed the Aleutian Island of Kiska and the threat to the Pacific Coast and Prince Rupert disappeared.

Armoured train personnel were released and some went on to serve overseas. In September 1943, the train was pulled to a siding at Terrace. The armament and equipment were removed and the armoured cars were decommissioned. August 1944 saw the No. 1 Armoured Train completely dismantled and components returned to the CN Railway. One year later, in August 1945, Japan surrendered, ending the war.

Nowadays, I ride the passenger train pretty often between Smithers and Prince Rupert. I always take notice of the Woodcock bunker with its massive cement walls and the leaning CN signpost "Tyee." I think about the armoured train lumbering down the tracks, and the soldiers who perched on top pointing guns with a fear we are so lucky to live without.

JAPANESE FIRE BALLOONS

During the final year of World War II, the Canadian army and American military attempted to silence rumours of an airborne threat floating over the Pacific Ocean from Japan. They reasoned that if the "enemy" did not know their weapons were successful, they would assume failure and cease launching the so-called "fire balloons."

The Japanese balloons, carrying incendiary and anti-personnel bombs, were meant to instill panic and cause fires and destruction when they randomly touched down. When airborne, the balloons were over seventy-five feet tall and thirty-five feet in diameter and capable of carrying just over two hundred pounds.

Captain Charles A. East described the balloons in the College of New Caledonia publication, *White Paper: Japanese War Balloons of World War Two*: "The balloon envelopes were made of five-ply laminations of very fine rice paper, pieced together in more than one hundred tapered segments." East wrote that over fifteen hundred feet of rope carried a chandelier rack suspending thirty-two sandbags of ballast and four incendiary bombs, with an anti-personnel bomb attached under the centre.

The balloons were inflated with hydrogen gas and sent off into the prevailing northwest winds of the upper atmosphere. They were ingeniously designed to drop a ballast bag when the balloon dropped in elevation, thus rising again and travelling farther. The balloon repeatedly lost and gained

This balloon, which came down near Babine Lake in 1945, carried several bombs that were defused and removed by Captain East and his team. Photo by C.A. East, courtesy of College of New Caledonia Press.

elevation, eventually dropping all its sandbags and falling randomly some-where on North America.

The Canadian military wanted no one to see the weapon: the balloons were to be recovered covertly by specially trained military personnel wearing protective gear and taking all steps necessary to remove the evidence. As a bomb-disposal officer stationed in Prince George, Captain East had a very busy year tracking down and disarming the Japanese paper balloons that landed in northern BC.

Captain East's first operation was to Takla Landing, in February 1945. This was the second balloon found in North America. After a harrowing flight on a ski-equipped Norseman aircraft, East and Corporal W.V.L. "Smitty" Smith hired Olaf Bjorinsen and his dog team to take them to the balloon crash site. The men camped on the Bear Lake winter trail under spruce trees and tolerated the howling of wolves. Captain East wrote that early in the morning they located the balloon caught on a pine snag and tangled over the top of sixteen other pines.

This was their first mission. They had been warned that a lightweight soldier may have been transported in the balloon as well, so they lay on their bellies and searched the site with binoculars. Both men thought the idea of a human surviving the journey and the landing very unlikely.

"Our instructions were that we were to wear coveralls, anti-gas boots, rubber gloves and surgical masks during the recovery operations," wrote East. He attempted to follow the rules, but the deep snow and hidden snags ripped his boots and tested his patience.

The two men managed to get the chandelier down. They bagged up samples and tried to remove the balloon from the treetops, but couldn't. Contrary to orders, they asked for help: William George, then seventeen, nimbly climbed the trees and tossed the balloon down. East told George that the balloons were Japanese and dangerous because he "… felt that it was safer for George to know the truth for his people, rather than have someone killed out of curiosity and incorrect information."

Just when the army thought the Japanese balloons were a well-kept secret, a full passenger train on the CNR line near Cedarvale witnessed a balloon drifting over the Skeena River. East and Smith were dispatched from Prince George, taking a jeep along the rough winter roads through Burns Lake, Houston and Smithers. After a short sleep there and an engine repair in Hazelton, the men went as far as the early road was ploughed, to Kitwanga. There they abandoned their vehicle, took a boat across the Skeena and a CN speeder car down the tracks, arriving late at night in Cedarvale where they were welcomed into the home of Mr. and Mrs. Essex.

In the morning, they crossed the Skeena and engaged Phillip Sutton to guide them up the Seven Sisters to where the balloon was last sighted. Sutton found the balloon "... suspended between three big trees, forming a huge canopy." East recalled that "a maze of ropes trailed down from it to the chandelier... two bombs were suspended opposite each other." East began walking around the balloon studying the circuits and the unexploded bombs when "... the heel of my snow-shoe snagged something and I looked at a black object projecting from the snow. With my hands I dug the snow from it to reveal the tail fins of a bomb."

Corporal Smith ascended the trees with climbing spurs, belt and rope. The men managed to untangle and gently lower the bombs where Captain East "... untapped the demolition charge and cut the fuse leading to the detonator." The anti-personnel bomb proved to be the biggest scare in Captain East's career. As he was holding the bomb in his hands and carefully using his special magnetic microphone and earphones, a branch falling from the treetops landed in the snow right behind him. After that scare, the men disarmed the bombs and packed all the evidence in Sutton's moose hides for the horses to pull down the mountain.

The Cedarvale balloon was shipped to "Defence Research" in New York to be studied.

Fort Babine on Babine Lake was Captain East's next mission and proved to be a recovery and destroy operation. The balloon was saturated with wet snow and was missing "the payload and controls." The evidence was burned. The army men stayed one night at the Fort Babine Hudson's Bay Company Store with store operator Bob Cunningham and his wife. Their exit from Fort Babine the next morning proved challenging—the ski-equipped air force plane had difficulty breaking free of the slushy ice and after five takeoff attempts Captain East was on his way.

This section of rope from the Cedarvale balloon was given to Mary Dalen, who has it on display at the Meanskinisht Museum in Cedarvale. More than 1,500 feet of rope went into the construction of each balloon. Photo by Jane Stevenson.

Captain East and his team disarmed balloons at Dome Creek, Collin Lake (southwest of Houston) and as far east as the Rauch Valley (near Valemount). Balloons landed at Barkerville, Fort Ware (at the head of the Finlay River), Chilako River, the Gang Ranch and Chilko Lake. Balloon fragments were found in Vanderhoof and were spotted near Quesnel, at the foot of Mount Robson and at Red Pass Junction near Jasper. In August 1945, one was reported at Pinchi Lake. Two other sightings turned out to be American weather balloons.

Captain East's last mission, to Goat River in October 1945, was a false alarm: the balloon turned out to be a split and folded-over tree with a large strip of bark fluttering in the breeze.

East describes this time of his life as exciting. He handled many Japanese bombs and escaped with no injuries. He says he may have been more than just skilled, more than just lucky: he ponders the fact that the bombs were never booby-trapped since the Japanese had the means to rig up tricks that would have proved fatal to anyone attempting to disarm a balloon. Germ warfare was also never part of the balloons, although military intelligence at the time considered it a threat. East "had the feeling these bombs were not meant to inflict horrific damage," and that the "enemy" was exercising restraint in its weaponry: "They [the balloons] were not the product of a savage war machine."

East commented that "There were no ribbons, medals or badges handed out to any of us, nor did we receive any special recognition for the fact that our small group was the only operational force of the army in Canada in actual contact with enemy operations on Canadian soil."

Captain East lived in Prince George for many years before retiring to Vernon. He died in January 1995.

MOVING THE NORTH:
THE BANDSTRA BROTHERS

John and Margaret Bandstra were married in Holland in spring 1951. Just two weeks later they packed their suitcases to board a ship bound for North America. John had been driving truck for a dairy company in Holland, but he wanted to do something on his own. "In those days, a fieldsman came to Holland and often talked about immigration to Canada," John recalls.

The fieldsman, Jacob Prins, had emigrated to Alberta in 1927 and was a strong advocate for Dutch settlement in the Edmonton area and in BC's Bulkley Valley. The idea of trying another country appealed to both John and Margaret. Margaret's brother had already moved to Smithers and from him they learned there were opportunities for new immigrants in the area.

They took a chance and sailed from Antwerp to New York City. During the ten-day passage, John and the other male passengers slept in the belly of the ship in swaying hammocks while Margaret stayed with the female passengers in the berths on the upper deck. From New York the couple made their way north, then by train across Canada to Smithers where they found a small but supportive Dutch community.

The Bandstras bought a small, rough-planked home just outside town for $600. John found a job driving truck from a small sawmill in the bush near Houston to the Duthie Mine on Hudson Bay Mountain. Margaret worked as a lumber-camp cook. Supplies for the camp were bumped over rough trails and the eggs were always broken. She shakes her head when she recalls the challenges; she was not used to Canadian food nor to the cooking. "But she caught on," smiles John.

Both Margaret and John had to learn English quickly while they worked. John learned the language by driving; he had to understand directions, freight measurements and amounts. He remembers how little English he knew when he first started: "When I wanted gas I had to pull up to the pumps and point. But I learned!"

Just four years after arriving, John teamed up with his brother Theo (who had immigrated to the area in 1952) and Andy Beerda to purchase Capling's Transfer, a Smithers-based general-delivery company. They saw potential in owning their own business and driving for themselves. John remembers his conversation with Capling about buying the business. When asked, "What assets do you have?" John replied, "I have a wife and three kids."

He also discussed the purchase with his wife. "I said to Margaret, 'I will be on the road at night. Should we do it?' And she said, 'Go for it. That is why we came, for the opportunity'."

Under the name Smithers Transport, the Bandstra brothers and Andy Beerda became the owners and operators of Capling's two single-axle trucks in 1955. They also became the drivers, mechanics, and warehousemen. Their main business at the time was shipping general freight between Smithers and Prince Rupert, including groceries, which at that time all came by boat to Rupert. The dockworkers who saw the new owners navigating the rough roads were skeptical, John remembers: "They said, 'I give these guys three months'."

Delivering groceries for the Goodacres' and Leach brothers' stores in Smithers became their steady business. John would often arrive in Smithers with a shipment early Saturday morning before the stores were open and recalls having to hunt someone down to open up for him so he could unload and go home.

Other freight kept them busy, too: "For quite a long time we hauled milk to Terrace and Rupert." They also dropped freight in the small communities along the way, including Trout Creek, Kitseguecla and Cedarvale. They picked up lumber at a sawmill in Usk ("all the lumber had to be hand-loaded, then hand-unloaded"), and on the return run from Rupert with groceries, the drivers picked up other freight when they could fit it in. They also hauled gas and sometimes dynamite for the Telkwa coal mines.

In 1955, it would take up to twelve hours to drive the 350 kilometres between Smithers and Rupert. "It was all bumpy roads, all gravel," says John. "Sometimes we even had boards along to cover a hole, then drive over it and pick up the boards again for the next hole down the road."

Conditions were so challenging, he says, that many times his was the only vehicle on the road between Smithers and Terrace. And when he did see another vehicle, it was often stuck. In the spring there was so much water on the road in places that the Smithers Transport trucks would pull smaller vehicles through. There were times when drivers were forced to lighten a truck by unloading it to get it out of a ditch or washout; then of course the freight all had to be reloaded.

The drivers went from Smithers to Rupert with stops between; they unloaded, took on the new freight and drove back. The long days of driving were a challenge, John recalls: "Sometimes I got out of the truck and I was so tired I didn't know if I came from Rupert or was heading to Rupert. Sometimes you tried everything—shoes off, stand in the snow—to stay awake."

The drivers were cautious but drove with confidence in the changing weather. The stretch between Rupert and Terrace was very narrow with rock walls on one side, railway tracks and river on the other. In winter, when CN ploughed the tracks, the heavy wet snow was pushed in huge piles onto the road. "Once, on the other side of Terrace, there was so much snow that the trucks were stuck from Thursday afternoon until Sunday morning. Even the graders got stuck. They had to bring bulldozers in from Prince Rupert."

John tells stories about washouts that could swallow a truck with ease. There were no radios in the early trucks, and usually no heaters. "If you had trouble shifting gears, you took the motor apart on the side of the road."

"They were young—they could do anything," Margaret says.

"We never gave up," says John.

The Bandstra truck frequently encountered challenging conditions while making their deliveries. This truck is mired in the mud on Babine Lake Road. Photo courtesy Bandstra Transportation.

The business grew. "Over the years we got more business, a few more trucks and more drivers," John recounts. Theo left to work in the automotive business and brother Dick (who had arrived in 1963) was brought in. The company remained competitive by expanding both in operations and area. They hauled freight and did general moving. They became a member of United Van Lines and operated a furniture van. There were major national and international shippers moving into northern BC and the Bandstras concentrated on exemplary service to set their business apart.

In 1971, a new warehouse and shop opened. Beerda was bought out and the Bandstra brothers, John and Dick, opened more terminals in northern BC, taking over smaller storage and moving companies in Houston, Terrace and Kitimat. In 1983, they opened a Vancouver division. They were operating under four different names at this time but in 1988 consolidated the company under Bandstra Transportation Systems.

John and his brother Dick have now retired, but the business is still very much family-run with their descendants taking the lead at the head office in Smithers and satellite offices throughout BC—"And now the grandchildren are coming to work for us."

"We made out alright," John reflects. With seventy-five trucks and two hundred employees under the company's wing, John must have displayed savvy business sense. But he places credit for its success elsewhere: "The one thing that always kept us going was our faith," he says. "We have been very blessed by the Lord."

NORTHERN BC'S

BROKEN ARROW

In September 1953, while searching for the missing aircraft of American millionaire Ellis Hall, a Royal Canadian Air Force search aircraft spotted a large debris field on the east side of the Kispiox Valley on Mount Kologet. The wreckage pointed to a large aircraft, with massive pieces of a plane spread out along the snowline at approximately six thousand feet elevation. This was the happenstance discovery of an American B-36 bomber that went missing in February 1950. After thousands of air time hours the search for Ellis Hall was called off. And the investigation of the American B-36 crash on a remote mountain top in the Kispiox Valley began.

On February 13, 1950, a massive United States Air Force B-36B strategic bomber #2705 carrying a crew of seventeen personnel sent out distress calls while flying south along British Columbia's coastline en route from Eielson Air Force Base, Alaska, to Carswell Air Force Base, Texas. The huge long-range bomber, with a wing span of over 230 feet, was flying a simulated combat mission during severe winter conditions. Aboard the plane was a bomb, a giant 10,000-pound Mark IV bomb, with a "dummy" capsule—meaning it had no plutonium core. While flying over Queen Charlotte Sound, the plane experienced engine fires, icing conditions

The survivors. Front row (left to right): Sergeant Ford, Corporal Schuler, Lieutenant Gerhart, Lieutenant MacDonald, Sergeant Stephens. Back row: Lieutenant Cox, Lieutenant Whitfield, Captain Barry, Sergeant Thrasher, Lieutenant Darrah. Copy of a *Vancouver Sun* newspaper clipping, courtesy of Bulkley Valley Museum Broken Arrow exhibit.

and instrument failure. Distress messages were sent out and the final message gave the failing plane's position as ninety miles south of Prince Rupert. Before jumping out of the plane, the radio operator Sergeant Trippodi tied down the transmitter key so the rescue crews could locate the plane and the survivors.

The area where the survivors jumped out of the doomed bomber was an isolated section of ocean and largely uninhabited islands. The weather in February was cold and the men were not expected to survive long, especially if they had landed in

An artifact from the B-36 crash site now on display at the Bulkley Valley Museum in Smithers, BC. Photo by Jane Stevenson.

the frigid ocean. Miraculously, on February 15, a fishing vessel spotted and saved survivors off Princess Royal Island. One man's parachute had become tangled in trees and he had dangled upside down for over twelve cold hours before being cut free. The same vessel found and retrieved three more survivors from their rubber life raft near Princess Royal Island. The search continued for weeks. Seventeen survivors in all were rescued. Five men were never found. The plane, it was assumed, had crashed in the ocean somewhere in Queen Charlotte Sound. According to the crewmen, the unarmed bomb was jettisoned from the plane before they abandoned the aircraft. This was possibly over Squally Channel or Estevan Sound. The crewmen reported a flash and large sound and shock waves as the bomb detonated upon contact with the water. (Because there was no plutonium core installed in the bomb, this was a non-nuclear explosion.) The US military chose to classify the B-36 bomber crash as a "Broken Arrow," a US Navy code word for an incident involving a nuclear weapon. The military also circulated the rumour that the aircraft crash site was located on the northern end of Vancouver Island.

In 1953, after the discovery of the B-36 bomber plane wreckage on Mount Kologet, the US Air Force was quick to get to the site before snow buried the evidence. They wanted to search the site, salvage any evidence and destroy the remains. This occurred during the Cold War and secrecy surrounded the mission. The Americans hired the Love brothers and Jack Lee, local horse guide outfitters, to take them up the rugged mountains. The team stayed at Marty Allen's ranch in the Kispiox Valley. The men ran into rough terrain and snow closed in on them in high elevations. In October, the team returned, unsuccessful. They made a few more attempts but eventually gave up, because this late in the season the bomber would be buried in snow. The salvage and destroy mission was resumed in August 1954 and this time the US Air Force used the Smithers Airport as their base. Smithers resident Hunter Simpson accompanied the men on this mission. The team spent nine days at the crash site. They salvaged electronics, radar and other sensitive materials before blowing up and destroying the remains of the plane.

How the crippled bomber ended up flying two hundred miles away from its estimated crash site in the Pacific Ocean and gaining over three thousand feet in altitude among the mountains of the Kispiox Valley remains a mystery. Some say one of the military men must have stayed on board and attempted to get the plane over the Canada-Alaska border to ensure the crash remained a domestic rather than an international incident. Subsequent researchers have also questioned whether or not the giant bomb was really dropped in the ocean and exploded on impact or if it went down with the plane. No one knows for certain. Many have pursued the question diligently for decades but found information requests from the USAF were not revealing. Dirk Septer published a thorough examination of the crash and the scenarios that may have led to it in his 2012 book, *Lost Nuke: The Last Flight of Bomber 075*.

Over the years the retreating summer snow on the mountain scree slopes revealed more of the plane, and in August 1997 a Department of National Defence and Environment Canada team conducted a survey of the crash site. They were searching the site for possible nuclear contamination. They found large portions of the plane still intact, including the tail section, propellers, a wing section and three engines. The team located unused explosives from the 1954 salvage and destroy mission as well as unexploded 20-mm canon shells and an aluminum box labelled "Explosives" that contained electronic detonators. Personal belongings including an airman's hat and pin were retrieved. The small blue pin reads "Mors ab alto," death from above. No radiation anomalies were detected.

The site became a publicly known crash site, and unfortunately looting of the site took place. Private individuals using helicopters removed artifacts from the crash site. Some items disappeared and remain in the hands of private collectors. A society was formed in Terrace with the intention of displaying some of the bomber crash site artifacts. Other items found their way into the displays and artifact storage areas of historical societies. The crash site is considered a historic site under BC Heritage legislation, and it is illegal to remove any objects from Mount Kologet. Every year there is increased summer snow melt and glacier retreat, so the site is changing. This also poses significant risk to people visiting the crash site because dangerous explosives and other hazards could be newly exposed. There are artifacts on display in exhibits at the Stewart Historical Society in Stewart, BC. The Bulkley Valley Museum in Smithers, BC, has a small permanent display containing an intimidating gun turret among other memorabilia. This display tells the amazing story of the discovery and mystery of the B-36 bomber in northern BC.

KITIMAT, BC

I grew up in Kitimat and didn't think anything of navigating the town according to the alphabetically arranged street names. I thought themed neighbourhoods were the norm, too. There were bird neighbourhoods with streets like Finch, Egret and Eagle, and fish neighbourhoods with Chinook, Char, Coho. Then there were river neighbourhoods—Skeena, Stikine, Yukon— and my childhood neighbourhood with "last name" streets like Stein, Swannell and Whittlesey.

I walked my dog on the lit and paved sidewalks that looped through town, under and over the roads. I learned to ride a bike on a smooth sidewalk with miles of mowed green grass on either side. Imagine my surprise when I moved to a city and was sprayed by road slush while I stood on the supposed sanctuary of the sidewalk. "Who the heck planned this city?" I would think. Certainly not Clarence Stein.

It was September 6, 1951, when Clarence B. Stein first landed in the Douglas Channel with a seaplane full of fellow planners. Stein was a sixty-nine-year-old architect from New York City, and he had flown to northern BC to see the muddy, rocky wilderness site where the new community of Kitimat was to be built.

Stein, along with town planners Mayer and Whittlesey, were hired by the Aluminum Company of Canada (Alcan, now called Rio Tinto Alcan) to design a master plan for the future townsite. In the early 1950s, Alcan was constructing a massive dam in the Nechako Valley, a ten-mile tunnel, a powerhouse, a fifty-mile

Topographer at plane table doing calculation in and for City Centre, November 10, 1953. Photo courtesy of Kitimat Museum and Archives, No. 73.3.4.5.

transmission line, an ocean terminal and an aluminum smelter. The company knew that the smelter required men and permanent housing in an attractive town and spared no expense in securing Clarence Stein and his team to plan a world-class community out of the one hundred square miles of allotted wilderness.

When Stein arrived on the shores of northern BC, there was no metropolis. For generations the Haisla First Nation had had a settlement (Kitamaat) where the Kitimat River flows into the Pacific, and there were once a few stalwart pioneer families scattered throughout the wide valley.

In the spring of 1951, the first construction crews arrived at the site of the future aluminum smelter. They cleared the land for bunkhouses and tents, built

Above: Prefabricated "Hullah houses" assembled on site in a Nechako neighbourhood in 1954. Photo by Fred Ryan, courtesy of Kitimat Museum and Archives, School District 80 Collection, No. 982.91.23. Opposite: Alcan on reconnaissance in May 1951. The men in charge of operations, from left: vice-president A.W. Whitaker Jr. in a helicopter used for aerial overviews during the planning process; project manager Percy E. Radley; chief resident engineer John Kendrick. Photo courtesy of Kitimat Museum and Archives, Kitimat Heritage Advisory Commission Collection.

tool sheds, cookhouses and a recreation hall. The building of a large aluminum smelter in northern BC was a mega-project and in every town and city people were talking about the industrial boomtown—the planned community of Kitimat. Hearing of the large-scale project, hundreds of men arrived by amphibious aircraft and later by the shipload.

These men built the smelter and the terminal as Stein and his team in New York planned every neighbourhood, street, home, school, shop, hydrant and even the cemetery. While the planners worked out the placement of schools and the size of the hospital, thousands of people from all over the world lived in temporary

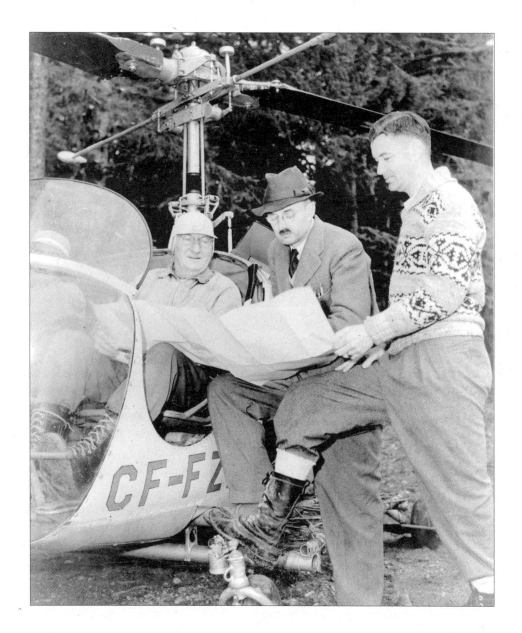

housing at the smelter site. Hundreds of men lived on the *Delta King*, a former California riverboat beached on the shore. "Married quarters" were established at the smelter site and a school was opened there in 1952. The school taught the workers' children in the day and taught English classes to the workers at night. One teacher, Mr. Bower, recalled that in one of his evening English classes of twenty-four students, fifteen European countries were represented.

Hundreds and soon thousands of men, women and children awaited the implementation of Stein's plan. They waited years for the design, construction and opening of the permanent schools, the large modern hospital, the shopping mall and for their brand new 1950s' homes.

Stein was the founder of the Regional Planning Association of America and an advocate of the "Garden City" concept. He planned pedestrian-friendly communities with looped streets, green spaces, low-density housing and room for expansion. For Kitimat, Stein planned a community where industry would be separated from the town centre and residential areas. Stein and his team also masterminded over twenty-eight miles of walkways, including pedestrian overpasses and underpasses, enabling connections to and from all areas of the community. Houses faced a common greenbelt and the designers took into account the needs of the town's residents. For example, they knew Kitimat would have a high proportion of shift workers, and laid out the houses with the master bedrooms away from the backyards where children would likely be making noise.

For each major neighbourhood, the planners accounted for pedestrian safety. Residents could walk to the nearest store and school by crossing a maximum of one road. The planners even purposely left "wild spaces" of untouched forest or open streams for the town children to play and learn in.

Maclean's magazine featured Kitimat in their May 1, 1954, issue. They noted that, "Most cities have been half smothered by the ailment of growing too big too fast, by narrow un-planned streets, traffic bottlenecks and widely sprawling housing developments without provisions for parks or playgrounds. Kitimat will be an exception. Alcan... spent close to a quarter of a million dollars designing the city on paper before the first nail was driven."

June 28, 1952. Land-clearing with a 5-ton steel ball, 8 feet in diameter, strung on a cable and pulled through the forest between two tractors. This method of tree clearing was limited to areas where trees did not exceed 12 to 14 inches in diameter. Photo courtesy of Kitimat Museum and Archives, No. 73.3.3.23.

In the summer of 1954, the first permanent residential neighbourhood, Nechako, was taking shape. There were approximately 450 houses ready by winter. There was a sense of permanence to the town as it left the temporary housing of the company town and became an independently run modern community.

Kitimat grew as retail outlets moved into the mall and other industries followed Alcan to the deep-sea port. The newly formed District of Kitimat supported the construction of a golf club, a rod and gun club, a YMCA, a movie theatre and a library. There were competitive soccer leagues, soapbox derbies, seasonal pageants, plays and even a pipe band. A railway was built between Kitimat and Terrace, and later a highway.

The planners imagined Kitimat would grow and allowed for a potential population as high as 50,000 people. The mall, hospital and schools were built to serve this predicted large population.

Kitimat was Stein's eighth and final planned community in the world, and the only one in Canada. He died in 1975 at the age of ninety-three.

Stein's vision has been adjusted over time. Houses have been renovated in ways that countered his design intentions and residents have fenced their patches of the greenbelt that Stein had pictured residents sharing as a common area. Due to the lower-than-predicted population, which peaked in 1982 at 13,482, schools have had to close and the hospital was demolished in favour of a new and smaller facility.

Stein's principal design features, those elements that are common in most garden cities, are still present and valuable today: the attractive community with frequent parks and open green spaces; the forty-five kilometres of lit and paved sidewalks; the separation of industry from residential areas.

Stein wrote in the July 1954 issue of *Architectural Digest* that he "… planned Kitimat with the intention that the physical plan would encourage interaction and foster the development of social cohesion and the capacity for the community to work together towards effective goals and remain resilient over time."

In recent times, Kitimat has suffered economic hardship followed quickly by economic investment. The community continues and, as Stein hoped, has remained resilient over time.

WALLY WEST

In 1932, sixteen-year-old W.D. "Wally" West walked down a back alley in Vancouver and came upon a row of photographic frames being exposed to daylight by a professional photographer. This was his first contact with the profession of photography, the profession he would excel in and pursue for the rest of his life.

In his autobiography, Wally explains that as a young man he tried selling vacuum cleaners and washing machines but had very little success. He wanted to be a photographer and at age nineteen he boldly approached a professional who was shooting several hundred music students on the stage of the Orpheum Theatre and asked to be his assistant. The photographer said yes—and so began Wally's education in the field.

The professional photographer, Mr. Sunday, and young Wally West developed a routine that went something like this: go wherever there was something happening, photograph the event, rush back to the rooming house bathroom, transform bathroom to darkroom, develop the prints, rush back to the event and make sales.

After capturing on film a banquet, a graduating class of nurses and a bowling tournament, Wally was set loose on his own to capture events and make sales. Using an 8×20 camera and a twenty-inch focal length lens, he "had to use the tilts and swings of [the] view camera to get depth of field." Wally learned through experience, hunting down events in the newspapers and guessing how many ounces of flash powder to use.

Children took to the streets of Prince George in 1947 to protest an increase in the price of Oh Henry bars from five to eight cents. They were successful, at least for the time being.

Photo by Wally West, courtesy of the Exploration Place, Wally West Collection, 993.11.1.79.3.

IWA Local 1-424 Christmas party in December 1953 during the longest strike in the area's history. Photo by Wally West, courtesy the Exploration Place, Wally West Collection, P1993.11.1.2301.6.

In his beginning years as an independent photographer, Wally developed prints in the lower berths of ferries and in abandoned sheds outside dance halls. He even learned to use the headlights of his car to develop prints. His hard work and talent was noticed, and in the late 1930s he was taken in by a professional photographer in Victoria.

It was in Victoria that West was asked to photograph the king and queen of England during their royal visit in 1939. Wally made his own reflector and wrapped cellophane over the flash bulbs and secured it with elastic bands. "In case," Wally explains, "the bulbs exploded the King and Queen would not get hurt." Wally used an 8×10 camera to photograph them and describes the event,

… the guests arrived and were seated. The royal party, The King and Queen followed by Lt. Governor Eric Hamber were seated. Now was the time to take the photograph, open the bulb shutter, press the connection to my bank of lights and then—boom—the bulbs with the cellophane exploded. This relieved the tension and the guests all started talking. The Queen expressed that this started everything off with a bang! Our location was near an alcove where the radio announcer was giving a report on the arrival of the Royal party. The explosion of the bulbs had been heard over the radio and President Roosevelt thought that the royal couple had been hurt. He telephoned to Victoria to inquire about the bang and the condition of the Royal party.

Wally West moved to Prince George in the fall of 1946, setting up a photographic studio in a dilapidated building downtown. Community members helped upgrade the nearly condemned building and his family moved in. W.D. West Studios opened just in time for Christmas portraits.

Wally had a knack for noticing a happening and capturing it with his camera. One of the first such events he shot in Prince George was a protest organized by South Fort George teacher Fanny Kenny. Her students were upset that the Prince George merchants raised the price of Oh Henry bars from five cents to eight cents. They rallied in the streets in a spontaneous protest and West photographed the spirited children marching in front of merchants' doorsteps. The stores listened and, for that year, held the price to five cents.

After four moves, W.D. West Studios established itself on Third Avenue. As a community photographer, West was often called out to photograph events in dimly lit community halls. Always up to a challenge, Wally would sequester himself in a nearby house, using the bathtub for the development and wash. He also built his own exposure box, with light bulbs in the bottom layers of glass where he could filter light with layers of tissue paper to the exposure box on top. Despite the dark halls, Wally managed to get everyone's face perfectly lit and the dim hall seemingly sunny.

Unusual circumstances gave rise to photographic discoveries. Prince George's cold winter weather presented challenges for taking perfect pictures until Wally learned to first warm up negatives with his hands. Residents coming to Wally for restoration of old family photos taken in "the old country" led to the invention of a custom magnifying and rotating touch-up table. An old 78-rpm turntable was used to rotate the photograph, which was held in place by a large metal pickle-jar lid with a hole cut in the top and backed with felt to protect the photo it held in place. An old car windshield-wiper flexed down to hold the lid in place and the precious photo still for the restoration work. Wally logged thousands of hours at this odd-looking table.

With determination and talent, Wally photographed both the everyday and the significant events throughout Prince George: the people, parades, corporate development, sporting events, portraits and scenic landscapes. The sports complex, the theatres, the various clubs and even heavy industry were all captured through his lens. Wally photographed the growth of Prince George over the decades, from the late 1940s to the 1980s. He had a real talent for capturing a scene and excelled in the darkroom.

Many hundreds of households in the Northwest must have a Wally West photo in their school albums or framed as a wedding portrait on their wall. West's talents were apparent in his first season of Christmas portraits and it was quite an occasion to have Wally himself show up to take your photo. W.D. West Studios became well known and possessed that certain mystique all businesses desire.

Wally received numerous awards and accolades in Canada and internationally, including the significant recognition by the Professional Photographers of Canada with an Honorary Master of Photographic Arts. Other recipients of this honorary award include Yousuf Karsh and the former Governor General of Canada, Roland Michener.

In 1991, Wally retired from his photography business and sold W.D. West Studios, which still operates to this day. Two years later, the City of Prince George purchased his massive collection of negatives and prints and donated them to the city's Exploration Place. Preserving over fifty thousand photographs, the museum provides a visual historical record of the City of Prince George in the Wally West Collection.

Wally West died in January 2008, at the age of ninety-two.

Newspaper carrier Walter Webster delivers the *Vancouver Daily Province* newspaper in the summer of 1950. The headline reads, "Korean Capital Falls, Canada to Send Aid." Photo by Wally West, courtesy of the Exploration Place, Wally West Collection, N1993.11.1.797.

Staff at the Exploration Place have logged many hours at their computers and scanners to put many of Wally West's distinctive photographs online, so you can see for yourself the talents of this great northern photographer.

1976 WILDCAT STRIKE

When a union goes on strike, things get tense. In Kitimat, at 6:00 am on June 23, 1976, the situation was ominous when riot squads unloaded from school buses and faced a picket line of union members from the Canadian Association of Smelter and Allied Workers. Shouting through megaphones, the police marched towards the picketers striking against the Aluminum Company of Canada (Alcan).

From the roof of the boiler building, employees at the Eurocan pulp-and-paper mill saw the RCMP riot squad already deployed, banging their shields with their riot clubs and advancing towards the picket line that the Alcan hourly workers had set up. The scene looked pretty intimidating, even from a distance. The union members—both men and women—standing by the picket-line fire-barrels and sitting on the log stumps blocking the road to the smelter were not there legally, and they knew it. But so deep was their dissatisfaction with their employer and with the federal government that they had spontaneously walked off the job in protest, starting a wildcat strike and illegal picket lines that lasted twenty-one days.

Kitimat was an industrial town and the hourly workers at the Alcan aluminum smelter had struggled to find a union that they felt represented their local and national interests. In the fall of 1972, they voted to form a new union and became the Canadian Aluminum Smelter and Allied Workers (CASAW). CASAW was

Members of the RCMP Tactical Unit during the illegal strike, June 1976. Photo courtesy of Kitimat Museum and Archives, Northern Sentinel Press Collection.

certified to be the local union for Alcan employees in October 1972 and had a small union hall in a trailer beside the Portuguese and Greek Clubs in Kitimat.

At issue for CASAW in 1976 was the federal government's perceived interference in the collective bargaining process between unions and their employers. Former Alcan worker Klaus Mueller Jr. explains that in 1975, Trudeau's federal Liberal government legislated wage and price controls in an effort to check the rapid rise in inflation: "Jean-Luc Pepin was the chairman of the anti-inflation board and they limited the amount of increases and limited the types of settlements that unions could negotiate." CASAW and other Canadian unions were upset that the government could overrule their negotiated settlements.

Because of high inflation rates, CASAW was stuck with a collective agreement in which wage increases were lower than inflation. It asked Alcan to re-open the contract, but this request was denied. Frustration towards the company and the federal government was building within the membership and throughout the smelter. Feelings of dissatisfaction rose to the point where the workers decided to walk out in a wildcat strike on June 2, 1976.

In the summer of 1976, Mueller was a young man working in potlining production services at the smelter, a department that repaired pots throughout the plant. In his job, he was able to sense the discontent bubbling throughout the plant. "The shop steward councils had met and there was lots of discussion about the discontent, but the union never sanctioned the walkout, never encouraged it. One by one, people came and went and got their work-mates," explains Mueller, "I was amazed at the unity—people who were non-radical were leading the walkout."

Picket lines were set up on the only road in and out of Alcan's smelter and at other places around the small town where supplies were flown or boated in. The strike received attention across the country and was featured on the national news.

A strike at the smelter can have huge consequences: if the aluminum is allowed to cool in the pots, the restart costs are enormous. Some feared the pots would solidify and the plant would never re-open because of the existing high inflation and low global demand for aluminum. The management team was asked to stay and maintain the pots, and some hourly employees chose to cross the picket line to assist them. The men and some women, derogatorily referred to as scabs, stayed in the plant, living there day and night to keep the smelter operating in a holding pattern. Necessary supplies were pushed in past picket lines and the smelter limped along without the majority of the eighteen hundred union workers.

Tensions ran so high that those who chose to scab were brought in by helicopter, or hidden in trucks or trunks of cars to get across the picket line. There were rumours of threats and vandalism directed at them. The un-sanctioned strike united the CASAW members, but their small community—neighbourhoods, churches, cultural groups and families—was deeply and bitterly divided.

CASAW dared to stand up to the federal government's perceived interference in collective bargaining and had great support from other Canadian unions, particularly those in Quebec. "Every union was watching this strike," says Mueller, "because it was the first real test of that government's wage and price control initiative, and because of the size of the workforce: 1,800 workers out for 21 days."

The strike was illegal and the BC Labour Board issued a cease-and-desist order, which the union ignored. The picket line was illegal because the strike was illegal and because the picket line was on Alcan's private road. When the riot squad was brought in on June 23, the picket line dispersed.

Lawyer Peter Burton, who in 1976 was the CASAW president, recalls that "the strike ended when a membership vote was tied on a motion to continue. Under the rules for union meetings, the President got to vote in those circumstances. I voted against the motion which meant that it was defeated, and the strike ended."

But the struggle didn't end when the picket lines came down and workers returned to the smelter. A headline in the *Terrace Herald* of July 21, 1976, reads, "Alcan Permitted to Discipline 136 Workers." The article states that Alcan applied to fire 31 employees it thought were instigators. The Labour Relations Board rejected this, instead allowing the suspension of 136 workers for varying lengths of time and the issuance of warning slips. For his part, then-president Burton was suspended for six months. He went on to become a lawyer specializing in labour relations.

Working separately from CASAW was the Canadian Labour Congress, which had its own strategies for fighting the wage and price controls. Some believe the wildcat strike in Kitimat played a role in stopping this program, which ended in 1978. According to Mueller, who quit working at Alcan shortly after the picket lines came down, the strike showed the government that this was not good legislation. "You have to know that there are times when you have to take a stand and fight for what is right," he says, "and then deal with the consequences."

SPANISH OLIVE JAR

When you step into the Masset Maritime Museum in Haida Gwaii, you see large-scale models of sailing ships, walls covered in nets, and exhibits of Pacific Ocean fishing and sea-faring life. There are cedar canoes and displays about the wooden-boat industry. Easily overlooked among the pretty glass fishing floats and shiny crab-canning machines is a modest glass case enclosing an eighteenth-century earthenware Spanish olive jar. According to lawyer Tom Beasley, whose hobbies include maritime history and underwater archaeology, this jar is the oldest known non-aboriginal artifact in British Columbia.

"In about 1986," Beasley says, "I wrote a letter to the editor of *Westcoast Mariner*, asking if any mariners or fishermen had dragged up pots in their nets." At the time, Beasley was researching early Chinese exploration on BC's west coast and was interested in ancient Chinese pots that had been dragged up from the deeps off Tofino.

Beasley's appeal resulted in a call from a fisherman. In the summer of 1987, Noel Stewart-Burton and crew were seining for salmon on the east coast of Langara Island, five hours by sea from the village of Masset. In their nets, from a depth of eight to ten fathoms (fifteen to eighteen metres), they had pulled a large, red-coloured earthenware jar about 75 centimetres by 40 centimetres in size.

The fisherman sent Beasley a photograph and a small piece of the jar that had broken off. The fragment went from the Underwater Archaeological Society of BC (UASBC) in Vancouver to the archaeology labs at Simon Fraser University.

There, David Huntley put the shard through a dating process known as thermoluminescence and determined that the jar was made some time between 1720 and 1790. Its distinctive shape, size, colour and material make-up helped them identify it as Spanish in origin.

"The jar," wrote Beasley (with Hector Williams, David Huntley and William Newton) in a 1993 *BC Studies* article, "is remarkably asymmetrical and seems to have been built up from separate sections that were thrown on the potter's wheel and then put together." Experts say the clay jar was a universal container—the eighteenth-century Spanish version of Rubbermaid bins—used for holding and transporting olive oil, wine, olives, figs, pickles, and even tar and soap.

Beasley said that the jar was a very significant find, and warranted an expedition to dive at the site to

Underwater archaeology and maritime history buff Tom Beasley stands beside the Spanish olive jar found off the coast of Haida Gwaii that dates back to the 1700s. Photo by Michael Paris, courtesy of the UASBC.

determine if there were other artifacts or possibly a shipwreck lying beneath the sea nearby.

Beasley and two other UASBC members—underwater photographer Mike Paris and UBC Professor of Mediterranean Archaeology Hector Williams—went to the site in 1990 to investigate. The team members were all divers. Williams, the academic of the group and one of the few professional underwater archaeologists then in the area, explains that when the Masset fishermen pulled up the jar they

Tom Beasley searches underwater for more artifacts near the site of the olive jar's discovery. Photo by Michael Paris, courtesy of the UASBC.

had taken a bearing from a dead tree onshore, so the team was able to return to the location of the discovery.

But they found nothing there. Beasley et al. wrote in *BC Studies* that "no further remains were discovered. The bottom area suitable for seining is relatively limited, as over much of the sea-bed there are large boulders. There is, however, a broad sandy stretch that possibly yielded the object. It may have been an accident of wave or current that exposed the toe or the broken upper end of the jar sufficiently to catch in the net as it dragged across the ocean floor."

Williams explains that a colleague working in Spanish archives discovered that there had been a Spanish ship near the northern end of Haida Gwaii during the date range of the discovered olive jar. Beasley further explains that the Spanish explorer Juan Perez had anchored in 1774 about a kilometre from where the jar was found. "Juan Perez on *Santiago* sighted land but was unable to put ashore because of adverse weather," says the *BC Studies* article, but some Haida paddled out to the *Santiago* and traded furs and other products for metal, trinkets, and old clothing. "In 1792, the Spanish returned under Jacinto Caamaño and erected a wooden cross more than six metres high at the north end of Graham Island across from Langara Island and close to the find spot of the jar."

Beasley and Williams can only guess how the jar came to be at the bottom of the Pacific, but admit that it is unlikely an unknown Spanish shipwreck awaits discovery in the area. More likely, the emptied or broken jar was thrown overboard from a Spanish ship as it passed or was anchored nearby. Also possible is that a non-Spanish vessel threw it out, or that the jar found its way into Haida hands and they jettisoned it themselves. Or it could have been moved by ocean currents over a long distance and deposited in the sands, only to be exposed enough in 1986 to snag in Noel Stewart-Burton's fishing nets.

Williams says the olive jar at the Masset Maritime Museum is significant because it is the only known Spanish artifact found in the waters off BC, and it offers a rare bit of evidence of the brief Spanish colonial presence on our shores. "But," says Beasley, "there are undoubtedly other similar and possibly older olive jars and pots elsewhere on the coast, as well as unknown pre-European-settlement shipwrecks waiting to be located." If there is another olive jar out there, maybe sitting in a fisherman's basement, let the Underwater Archaeological Society of BC know about it. They are keen to get in the ocean again and discover more clues about the early exploration of coastal British Columbia.

BRIDGE BACK IN TIME

About seven miles up the Bulkley River from Telkwa, in the rural community of Quick, there is a single-lane wooden bridge with long fir timbers spanning the three-hundred-foot crossing. This bridge, commonly known as the Quick Bridge, was built in 1921 and is one of fewer than seven wooden Howe truss bridges remaining north of Quesnel.

William Howe came from a family of inventors in Massachusetts and patented the Howe truss in 1840. In the autumn of 2010, Ministry of Transportation and Infrastructure (MoT) Regional Bridge Engineer Ed Cienciala explained that Howe truss bridges are easily identified because they have upper and lower chords with distinctive triangulation of cross-members. He pointed out that Howe truss bridges were once popular, and often favoured by railways, because they easily covered long spans and could carry a heavy load.

Cienciala agreed that the Quick Bridge is exceptional because it was built in place in 1921 and has, remarkably, survived over ninety years of traffic—horses and wagons to cars and trucks—and survived the extremes of the river—ice jams and floods.

The rural district of Quick was settled by farmers who had grain and produce to export and breeding stock and farm machinery to import. The Grand Trunk Pacific Railway was built along the west bank of the Bulkley River upstream from Telkwa in the summer of 1913. Unfortunately for the majority of established farmers there, the railway was on the opposite side of the river from their farms.

Before the Quick Bridge was constructed, farmers who needed to cross the Bulkley River with their loaded wagons were forced to travel all the way to Hubert, a short-lived settlement not far from Telkwa where a low-level Howe truss bridge had been built in 1914. The *Omenica Herald* of New Hazelton reported that residents of the Quick area had to travel great distances just to collect their mail. "It necessitated trips sometimes over 30 miles return, when the opportunity could be found to make the trip, which usually meant weeks or even months between." There was also a cable ferry crossing the Bulkley River at Walcott and some farmers reached the railway by using this ferry—also a lengthy trip.

An ice jam in January 1919 took out two spans of the Hubert Bridge, and this crossing was never replaced. Instead the Public Works Department decided to build a new bridge upstream. The Quick Howe truss bridge was built in 1920 and 1921 on three concrete piers with its base well above the winter water levels. The critical bottom chord was made of two sets of 180-foot-long fir beams placed end-to-end to run the length of the bridge and support the entire structure. In 1921, the *Smithers Interior News* reported that "work on the Quick Bridge is progressing quite favourably. This no doubt will prove of great value to this neighbourhood as it will enable the farmers loading hay to make two trips a day."

That same year, entrepreneur Wadham Locke Paddon purchased land near the river crossing on the railway side of the Bulkley to build a general store and supply depot. With the help of Mr. Long Sing, Paddon built a store right beside the newly completed Quick Bridge. At first he sold feed to the area's farmers, but by 1923 he had established his rural store as a source of dry goods, hardware, tack, farm implements and tools, and even weather information.

The winter of 1923 also saw postal service established for the area, at the Quick railway station by the new bridge. The *Omenica Herald* reported that residents welcomed the progress and were happy to see Mr. Bruff out in the piles of snow building a "catch-post" (or "mail crane") that allowed passing trains to pick up the bags of mail hanging from it.

The Quick Bridge was a crucial commercial link between the farmers and the railway. Passengers could also come and go from Quick—farm labourers often

The old bridge at Hubert, which had a sweeping, curved approach, was taken out by ice in 1919 and never replaced. Photo courtesy of Telkwa Museum, P0155.

arrived in large numbers to help at harvest time. Manufactured goods came in by rail; farm produce, railway ties, vegetables and grain went out. In the 1940s, tons of locally grown potatoes were hand-loaded at the Quick Station into refrigerated railway cars for shipment to Prince Rupert.

In the 1940s, the Yellowhead Highway usurped the rails as the chosen transportation method. The train stopped less and less often, then not at all. The Quick Bridge saw less traffic. At the Quick store, Paddon's business gradually slowed but never quite stopped.

Dave and Bridget Gillespie bought Paddon's store on the corner of Quick Station Road and Paddon Avenue in 1976. They renovated the buildings into a family home and raised their two girls in the old store. From their home by the Bulkley River, or from higher and drier ground, they've witnessed the old bridge

Construction of the Hubert Bridge. Smoke rises across Bulkley River as settlers clear the land. Photo courtesy of Telkwa Museum, P0158.

survive ice jams and floods in 1984, 2005 and 2009. These were not the first times: ice jams had threatened the bridge in 1930, 1936 and 1939 as well, and significant high waters flooded the area in 1949 and 1966.

The many years of regular use and stress from ice and high water have caused definite wear and tear on the structure. Over the decades, the Ministry of Transportation has carried out major repairs and significant structural improvements: a new approach was built, joists and decking were replaced, and the trusses and concrete piers were repaired. The load limit was lowered to eight tonnes to guarantee the security of the bridge and the safety of those people using it.

In 2011, the MoT's inspection revealed that the bridge is ageing—they found pockets of rot in the fir timbers that make up the bridge's crucial bottom chord. Even though it is wearing slightly with age, the Howe truss bridge poses no current danger to users and continues to be a safe route across the Bulkley River for both vehicles and pedestrians—as long as the posted load limit is obeyed. Ministry officials

Paddon's Store

Bob Fraser was seventeen years old in 1953 when he left his home in Scotland and came to work in Quick cutting and hauling ties. Fraser worked for Mr. Paddon hauling ties that had been hacked by broad axe by other workers. Tie cutting represented important seasonal work for the famers all through the Bulkley Valley. Many farming men and sons (and occasionally wives and daughters, too) headed to the hills to cut trees down to length and shape them with a broad axe so they became railroad ties for the track to run on. Paddon recalls that some of the young workers were from Saskatchewan; others were local First Nations men. "I hauled the ties with Mr. Paddon's team of horses and a sleigh," says Fraser. The ties were brought to the siding at Quick Station where they were piled up. When the ties were piled high enough to fill a boxcar, the CNR train would stop and a boxcar would be loaded full of the hand-hewn ties. Fraser describes 1953 Quick as "stepping back in time." "The Paddon's," says Fraser, "had a well by the house with a hand pump and an outdoor toilet." In 2011, Fraser reminisced about the Quick community and said he liked Quick and made friends with fellow teenagers living on farms there. He is still friends with them today.

explain that to address the problem the bottom chords may have to be removed and replaced—and to do this the entire structure will need to be dismantled.

The Gillespies and many other area residents would like to see efforts continue to repair and ultimately preserve their old Howe truss bridge. The MoT has heard these concerns but points out that it would be a long, difficult and expensive process to rebuild the wooden bridge, adding that if a new wooden Howe truss bridge were to be built there, the wood for the lower chords would be very difficult to find and would likely be preservative-treated and glue-laminated. MoT prefers the option of removing the Howe truss and replacing it with a modern crossing. Although Cienciala acknowledged that it would be a shame if another historic crossing such as the Quick Bridge had to come down, ultimately, a safe long-term crossing is needed.

The residents of Quick have seen their little railway station get taken down and their school close. They are hoping to see the Howe truss bridge, one of Quick's last local historic structures, remain. MoT plans to work with residents to ensure they have a crossing and that their crossing is safe. As of winter 2012, the old Quick Howe truss bridge remains over the Bulkley River in Quick, BC.

NORTHERN MEMORY PLACES

Historians tend to view their surroundings from the perspective of not just what is here now and what might be here in the future, but also what was once there: an abandoned village site, a forgotten town, a manned lighthouse. Those of us who study local history have "memory places" that date back far beyond our short lifetimes. I absorb historical details that people share with me and it changes the way I look at the passing landscapes outside the train, the car, the boat, and so on.

There are those in the Northwest of our province who spend their days examining artifacts, cataloguing items, and actively researching our past. I asked some of these people to consider their towns and the unmarked historic places that exist throughout the landscape, then describe one site they associate with their town's unique history.

Over 100 years old, Prince Rupert is rich with official historic sites. When asked what unmarked site holds special local historical significance for her, Jean Eiers-Page, archivist at the Prince Rupert City and Regional Archives, considered first the World War II Barrett Fort and the important Lucy Island Lighthouse before finally settling on Salt Lake. "Salt Lake is located on the mainland at the end of Russell Arm, across the harbour from Prince Rupert," she explains. It is called Salt Lake because during very high tides, ocean salt water spills into the lake. Between these tidal events, the water warms and makes for ideal swimming.

SALT LAKE P. RUPERT B.C AUG 3. 1919

W.W.W. PHOTO.

Prince Rupert's natural saltwater swimming spot, Salt Lake, was a very popular recreation destination in the city's early days. Photo courtesy of Prince Rupert City and Regional Archives, Museum of Northern BC Collection, Wrathall Collection, WP997.44.12884.

Eiers–Page explains that this off-the-beaten-path site was once a popular local swimming and recreation spot—so popular there was even a ferry that ran people across from the city. "In the early days of Prince Rupert the locals travelled across the harbour to swim, picnic, stay in cabins and skate in the winter," she recalls. From archival photographs, Eiers-Page describes the site: "There was a dock and a change room, and a floating dock with five diving platforms was built in the 1920s." Once an outdoor pool was built in Rupert, and the highway to the east opened up other swimming locations, the popularity of Salt Lake declined. An indoor pool opened in 1958, further diminishing Salt Lake's recreational appeal.

Kitimat Museum and Archives curator Louise Avery nominates the historic vista locally known as "the Viewpoint," along with the view of the Douglas Channel. "Together, they are Kitimat's most defining natural features," she says. The Viewpoint is located along the long Haisla Hill as you descend into

The old Reo Theatre, now renamed the Grand Reo, still stands in Vanderhoof and still shows movies. Photo courtesy of Kevin Wallace.

Kitimat by road; there is a pull-out and a little public park where the ocean and Douglas Channel come into view. Avery explains that the Douglas Channel was referenced by several explorers dating back to the late 1700s and was central to Haisla Nation activities over the centuries. The Viewpoint had special significance for the Haisla, because it was one of the sites from which they could spot raiding parties coming up the channel.

"In the late 1940s, the location of the Kitimat Project was chosen because of the juxtaposition of this tide-water and the hydroelectric power source," says Avery. Douglas Channel, as seen from the Viewpoint, is a significant memory place.

Laurel Smith Wilson, executive director and curator of the 'Ksan Historical Village and Museum in Hazelton, says the riverboat landing in downtown Old Hazelton carries special significance both for local history and for her personally. "My maternal grandmother was born in 1898, so she was a young child when the riverboats were running the Skeena. I recall her saying the riverboats would blow their whistles far off downriver to announce their approach." She said that all the Hazelton residents, including herself, would run down to the landing to greet the strangers coming off the boat. "We were so curious and eager to see new faces." The boats stopped running the river in 1912, but you can visit the boardwalk that runs along the Skeena River in Hazelton today to experience Smith Wilson's memory place.

Lee Safonoff has been the curator at the Lakes District Museum for at least twenty-four years. The local landmark she thinks holds interesting historical significance is largely unknown and certainly unmarked. In the Burns Lake Cemetery lies "Buckskin Jim," known to locals as Herbert James Atkinson. "He was born in Michigan in 1858," says Safonoff. "He was associated with Custer and was a friend of Buffalo Bill." Buckskin Jim is known throughout the US, with monuments erected to his memory in a number of different states, but in Burns Lake his grave is unmarked. Safonoff explains that Buckskin Jim lived (as James Atkinson) at François Lake until he died in 1932, with arrow and bullet wounds evident on his body. "There is no monument on his grave, but those who like history and the thrill of the find will like this little-known historical site." If you visit the Lakes District Museum, Safonoff will draw you a map and send you to the right section of the town cemetery to visit the grave of Buckskin Jim.

At the Vanderhoof Community Museum, manager and curator Heather Stephens considers carefully the sites that once were: where a granary once stood, where a railway station once was, where a telegraph line once ran. After much thought, she chooses a site that still exists. "The Grand Reo Theatre on Burrard Avenue is an interesting historical landmark. It is like stepping back in Vanderhoof's history; you can't help but recall the past." The tall and flat-roofed building, built more than ninety years ago and originally operated as the Reo, still carries on as a small, family-run community theatre today. Stephens has enjoyed seeing the theatre advertisements in old newspapers and cites the theatre as a significant but undeclared community historic site.

Ramona Rose, head of Archives and Special Collections at UNBC, when asked what historical landmark is often overlooked, says, "my vote is for the cutbanks along the Nechako River." She points out that, "This geographic feature has witnessed the growth and development of what is now Prince George. The cutbanks have seen bridges being built and torn down, paddlewheelers and scows plying up and down the Nechako River." You can't miss Rose's memory place as you drive into Prince George from the east and the south and along the length of the Nechako.

All of us have memories that are linked to physical sites—the street you grew up on, the place you first learned to swim. The life events associated with your personal history make up your memory places. Share these with each other and change the way we view our Northwest.

REFERENCES

Numerous sources contributed to the creation of this book. Wherever possible the people I interviewed were credited in their stories. Many families shared their personal stories with me and generously allowed me access to their photo albums and family papers. Businesses and various government departments also allowed access to their maps and records. Thank you!

The following books and archival materials were consulted:

Asante, Nadine. *The History of Terrace*. Terrace, BC: Totem Press, 1972.

Ball, Fay et al. *Pioneer Women*. Smithers, BC: Bulkley Tweedsmuir Women's Institute, 1967.

Barman, Jean. *The West Beyond the West: A History of British Columbia*. Toronto: University of Toronto Press, 1996.

Bennett, Norma V. *Pioneer Legacy: Chronicles of the Lower Skeena*. 2 volumes. Terrace, BC: Dr. R.E.M. Lee Foundation, 1997–2000.

Bowman, Phyllis. *Whistling through the West*. Prince Rupert, BC: P. Bowman, 1980.

Burns, Walter T. *Dominion Experimental Farm Substation Report: 1938–1950, Smithers, British Columbia*. Ottawa: Department of Agriculture, no date.

Carmichael, Alfred. "Account of a Season's Work at a Salmon Cannery – 1891 – Windsor Cannery, Aberdeen, Skeena." *Skeena Digest*, Volume 2, No 1, Spring 1970.

Coulsen, Mel. *Skypilot Stephenson In His Own Write: A Biographical Sketch based on Rev. F.L. Stephenson's Own Writings*. Telkwa, BC: May 2010.

Department of Colonization and Agriculture. *Photographs and Data on Settlement in the Burns Lake District*. Winnipeg, Manitoba: Department of Colonization and Agriculture, 1940.

Dickie, Francis. "New York – Siberia; The Astonishing Hike of Lillian Alling." In *Pioneer Days in British Columbia*, edited by Art Downs, volume 2, 140–145.

Downs, Art. *Paddlewheels on the Frontier, The Story of British Columbia and Yukon Sternwheel Steamers*. University of Michigan, Superior Publishing Company, 1972.

Downs, Art, ed. *Pioneer Days in British Columbia: A Selection of Historical Articles from BC Outdoors Magazine*. Volumes 1, 3. *BC Outdoors*, 1973–77.

Downs, Art, ed. *Pioneer Days in British Columbia: A Selection of Historical Articles from BC Outdoors Magazine*. Volumes 2, 4. Nanoose Bay, BC: Heritage House, 1975–79.

East, Captain Charles A. *White Paper: Japanese War Balloons of World War Two*. Prince George, BC: College of New Caledonia, 1993.

Fraser Lake and District Historical Society. *Deeper Roots and Greener Valleys*. Fraser Lake, BC: Fraser Lake District Historical Society, 1986.

French, C.H. and W. Ware. "BC Post: The Hazelton Post." *The Beaver*, May 1924.

Glen, J. Sr. *Where the Rivers Meet: The Story of the Settlement of the Bulkley Valley*. Duncan, BC: New Rapier Press, 1977.

Grand Trunk Pacific. *Smithers, GTP Freight and Divisional Headquarters*. 1914. Reprint, Smithers, Bulkley Valley Historical and Museum Society, 1979.

Gottesfeld, Allen S. and Ken A. Rabnett. *Skeena River Fish and their Habitat*. Hazelton, BC: Skeena Fisheries Commission and Portland, OR: EcoTrust, 2008.

Horetzky, Charles. *Canada On The Pacific: Being An Account of the Journey From Edmonton to the Pacific By the Peace River Valley and A Winter Voyage Along the Western Coast With Remarks to the Physical Features of the Pacific Railway Route and Notices of the Indian Tribes of British Columbia*. Montreal: Dawson Brothers Publishing, 1874.

Kruisslebrink, Harry. *Smithers: A Railroad Town*. Smithers, BC: Bulkley Valley Historical and Museum Society, 2008.

Large, Dr. R. Geddes. *The Skeena: River of Destiny*. Vancouver, BC: Mitchell Press, 1957.

Lawrence, Guy. "Yukon Telegraph." *British Columbia Digest Magazine of Outdoor British Columbia*, Volume 17, No 5, October 1961, 14–21.

Leach, Norman S. *Broken Arrow: America's First Lost Nuclear Weapon*. Calgary, AB: Red Deer Press, 2008.

Leonard, Frank. *A Thousand Blunders: The Grand Trunk Pacific Railway Company and Northern British Columbia*. Vancouver: UBC Press, 1996.

Lindstrom, Emma A. *From Riverboats to Railroads*. Terrace, BC: Regional Museum Society, 1992.

Lower, J.W. "The Construction of the Grand Trunk Pacific Railway in British Columbia." *British Columbia Historical Quarterly* 4 (1940), 163–181.

MacDonald, James M. "Bleeding Day and Night: The Construction of the Grand Trunk Pacific Railway Across Tsimshian Reserve Lands." *Canadian Journal of Native Studies* 10 (1990), 33–69.

McHarg, Sandra and Maureen Cassidy. *Before Roads and Rails: Pack Trails and Packing in the Upper Skeena Area*. Hazelton, BC: Northwest Community College, 1980.

Miller, Bill. *Wires Through the Wilderness; The Story of the Yukon Telegraph*. Surrey, BC: Heritage House, 2004.

Mitcham, Allison. *Atlin, The Last Utopia*. Hantsport, Nova Scotia: Lancelot Press, 1989.

Mould, Jack. *Stumpfarms and Broadaxe*. Saanichton, BC: Hancock House, 1976.

Newman, Ken. "Dorreen, Telegraph Trail." Unpublished research paper. Terrace, BC: Regional District of Kitimat Stikine, 2012.

Olds, Charles Sr. *Looking Back, Down Time and Track*. Prince George: privately printed, 1973.

O'Neill, W.J. "Wiggs." *Steamboat Days on the Skeena River.* Kitimat, BC: Northern Sentinel Press, 1960.

Orchard, Imbert. *Martin: The Story of a Young Fur Trader.* Sound Heritage Series, no. 30. Victoria: Provincial Archives of British Columbia, 1981.

Pauls, Helen Rose. "The Way We Were; The First Mennonite Church, Burns Lake, BC." *Roots and Branches: Newsletter of the Mennonite Historical Society of BC,* 14:1, January 2008, 18–19.

Prince Rupert City and Regional Archives. *Prince Rupert: An Illustrated History.* Prince Rupert, BC: Prince Rupert City and Regional Archives, 2010.

Pybus, Cassandra. *The Woman Who Walked to Russia: A Writer's Search For a Lost Legend.* Markham, Ontario: Thomas Allen & Sons Ltd., 2002.

Roseburg, Marjorie ed. *Bulkley Valley Stories, Collected From Oldtimers Who Remember.* Smithers, BC: Heritage Club, 1973.

Rutstrum, Calvin. *Hiking Back to Health.* Pittsboro, IN, Indiana Camp Supply, 1980.

Septer, Dirk. *Lost Nuke: The Last Flight of Bomber 075.* Victoria: Heritage House Publishing, 2012.

Shervill, Lynn. *Smithers; From Swamp to Village.* Smithers, BC: Town of Smithers, 1981.

Shervill, Lynn. "Have You Ever Wondered… Who Invented the Egg Carton?" *BC Historical News,* Spring 1982, 22–23.

Skogan, Joan. *Skeena, A River Remembered.* Vancouver: BC Packers Ltd., 1983.

Smedley-L'heureux, Audrey. *Northern BC in Retrospect.* Volume 1. Vanderhoof, BC: 1979.

Stevenson, Jane. *The Railroader's Wife: Letters from The Grand Trunk Pacific Railway.* Halfmoon Bay, BC: Caitlin Press, 2010.

Stoesz, Conrad. "Migration to Burns Lake BC, 1940." *Mennonite Historian,* 29:1, March 2003.

Talbott, F.A. *A New Garden of Canada, By Pack-horse and Canoe Through Undeveloped New British Columbia.* London, New York and Melbourne: Cassell and Company Ltd., 1911.

Terrace Regional Historical Society. *Seventy-five Years of Growth.* Terrace, BC: Whitecap Books, 1981.

Turkki, P. *Burns Lake and District, A History Formal and Informal.* Burns Lake, BC: Burns Lake Historical Society, 1973.

Wearne, Hilary. *Pioneer Women.* Smithers, BC: Bulkley Tweedsmuir Women's Institute, 1967.

Weedmark, Lillian. *Pioneer Women of the Bulkley Valley.* Smithers, BC: Bulkley Valley Historical and Museum Society, 1995.

Weedmark, Lillian. Remember When (series). *Interior News,* 1992–1994.

West, Wally. *Autobiography: Wally West's History of Photography.* Prince George, BC: Fraser Fort George Museum Society, no date.

Wicks, Walter. *Memories of the Skeena.* Saanichton, BC: Hancock House, 1976.

Wicks, Walter. "Early Gillnet Fisherman." In *Pioneer Days in British Columbia: A Selection of Historical Articles from BC Outdoors Magazine,* edited by Art Downs, Volume 2, 76–80. Nanoose Bay, BC: Heritage House, 1975–79.

Williams, Hector, Tom Beasley, David Huntley and William Newton. "Research Notes: An 18th
    Century Olive Jar from the Queen Charlotte Islands." *BC Studies* 96, Winter 1992–1993, 90–99.

The following collections were consulted:

Bandstra Transportation Systems, Smithers, BC
BC Archives, Victoria, BC
Bulkley Valley Museum, Smithers, BC
Burns Lake Museum, Burns Lake, BC
College of New Caledonia, Prince George, BC
Hazelton Pioneer Museum, Hazelton, BC
Kitimat Centennial Museum, Kitimat, BC
K'san Historical Village and Museum, Hazelton, BC
Lakes District Museum, Burns Lake, BC
Massett Maritime Museum, Masset, Haida Gwaii, BC
Meanskinisht Museum, Cedarvale, BC
Mennonite Heritage Centre, Manitoba
Northwest Community College, Terrace and Smithers campuses, BC
Prince George Exploration Place, Prince George, BC
Prince George Railway and Forestry Museum, Prince George, BC
Prince Rupert City and Regional Archives. Prince Rupert, BC
Prince Rupert Library, Prince Rupert, BC
Telkwa Museum, Telkwa, BC
Terrace Public Library, Terrace, BC
Transcona Historical Museum, Winnipeg, MB
Underwater Archaeological Society of BC, Simon Fraser University, Burnaby, BC
University of Northern BC, Archives and Special Collections, Prince George, BC
Valley Museum and Archives, McBride, BC
Vanderhoof Community Museum, Vanderhoof, BC

The following newspapers were consulted:

*British Colonist, Colonist, Hazelton Queek, Interior Dairy Guide, Interior News, Kitimat Sentinel, Omenica
    Herald, Omenica Miner, The Province, Prince Rupert Empire, Terrace Herald, Whitehorse Star.*

INDEX